Library of
Davidson College

HAITI AND THE UNITED STATES

Also by J. Michael Dash

JACQUES STEPHEN ALEXIS
LITERATURE AND IDEOLOGY IN HAITI, 1915–1961
THE RIPENING (A translation of *La Lezarde* by E. Glissant)

Haiti and the United States

National Stereotypes and the Literary Imagination

J. Michael Dash
Senior Lecturer in French
University of the West Indies

St. Martin's Press   New York

© J. Michael Dash 1988

All rights reserved. For information, write:
Scholarly and Reference Division,
St. Martin's Press, Inc., 175 Fifth Avenue, New York, NY 10010

First published in the United States of America in 1988

Printed in Hong Kong

ISBN 0-312-01684-0

Library of Congress Cataloging-in-Publication Data
Dash, J. Michael.
Haiti and the United States: national stereotypes and the
literary imagination/J. Michael Dash.
p.   cm.
Bibliography: p.
Includes index.
ISBN 0-312-01684-0: $30.00 (est.)
1. Haitian literature—History and criticism. 2. Haitian
literature—American influences. 3. American literature—History
and criticism. 4. Haiti in literature. 5. United States in
literature. 6. Haiti—Relations—United States. 7. United States—
Relations—Haiti. 8. National characteristics in literature.
I. Title.
PQ3948.5.H2D37   1988
840'.9—dc19   87-32912
                                                                  CIP

To Miss Lauren Who
'Jes Grew'

Contents

Preface ix
Acknowledgements xii
Chronology xiii

1 Through the Eyes of the Other: Stereotypes of the Nineteenth Century 1

2 Through the Looking Glass: Textual Politics and the American Occupation 22

3 Dreaming the Same Dream: Harlem, Haiti and Racial Solidarity 45

4 Passionate Apologists: Haiti and the United States in the Post-Occupation Years 73

5 The Art of Darkness: Writing in the Duvalier Years 101

6 Epilogue: Caribbean Overtures 135

Notes 140
Index 149

Preface

> Images were first made to conjure up the appearances of something that was absent. Gradually it became evident that an image could outlast what it represented.
>
> John Berger, *Ways of Seeing*
>
> Fiction never lies.
>
> V. S. Naipaul, *The Killings in Trinidad*

The United States invaded Haiti in an aggressive, military fashion in 1915 and initiated an intense relationship between the two republics that exists up to the present. Even though 1915 meant the violent entry of the United States into the Haitian experience and vice versa, the preceding decades reveal an awareness of the United States among Haitian intellectuals. The latter were, admittedly, more concerned with European culture but towards the end of the nineteenth century there is clear concern with American expansionism. After 1915, with the increased visibility of Americans in Haiti, attitudes to the United States are more widespread and clearly defined. There was also great interest shown in Haiti by American writers, travellers and later anthropologists. This study sets out to trace the growth and nature of this contact in both Haitian and American writers. This includes the sensationalism of the Occupation period, the link with Afro-American writers, the more informed work of American anthropologists and the Duvalier dictatorship which until recently shocked and titillated Americans. With the fall of the Duvalier dynasty the relationship between Americans and Haitians is more intense than ever before.

This study is an attempt to eavesdrop on an intense and often heated dialogue that has been sustained between Haiti and the United States – two New World Republics whose origins are remarkably similar but whose destinies are startlingly different. This passionate exchange is traced not in official documents or diplomatic correspondence but in works of fiction, travel books and imaginative literature in general. Attitudes and stereotypes that are either cautiously handled or camouflaged by claims of objectivity in historical or socio-political works, emerge with a disarming honesty in less high-minded documents. The simplistic paternalism of a marine's memoirs, the supercilious chauvinism of a nineteenth century Haitian visitor to the United States, the taste for the outlandish among negrophile Americans reveal an unofficial truth about Haitian–American relations and go a far way towards creating stereotypes that have an influence on national policy and official reactions.

The main contention here is that a study of these narratives offers a useful perspective on Haitian–American relations which is not always available through traditional methods of historical investigation. Both Haitian and American attitudes cannot always be understood unless we are aware of the imaginative and even linguistic constraints within which they operate. The fictions of a given period are a key to the emotional underpinnings for an official policy, a framework within which even historical narrative can be explained. In blurring the difference between fiction and non-fiction, in treating fiction with the seriousness normally reserved for non-fiction, this study attempts to capture the hidden discourse behind official attitudes. The travel writer's choice of anecdote, the novelist's description of protagonists, the poet's terminology not only affect the way we think and feel but, even when new situations present themselves, we are tempted to recall and dwell on stereotypes which have never really vanished. They remain deeply embedded in the unconscious and give shape and direction to fresh experiences that flood the mind.

The aim is not so much to provide an exhaustive history of literary contacts between Haiti and the United States nor to supply an endless inventory of books in which Americans discuss Haiti and vice versa. Some attempt to do precisely this can be found in the following articles: Y. Gindine, 'Images of the American in Haitian Literature during the Occupation', *Caribbean Studies*, vol. 14, no. 3 (1974); M. Fabre, 'Le revue indigène et le mouvement nouveau noir', *Revue de Litterature Comparée*, no. 1 (Jan.–Mar. 1977); L.-F. Hoffmann, 'Les Etats-Unis et les Americains dans les lettres haitiennes', *Etudes Littéraires*, vol. 13, no. 2 (1980) and in Fleischmann, *Ideologie und Wirklichkeit in der Literatur Haitis* (1969). Instead, this is an attempt to show how polarizing stereotypes in imaginative literature are developed which make historical and political realities intelligible. In the case of Haiti and the United

States it means producing myths which make the other's existence more manageable, less threatening.

In attempting to classify and analyse the imaginative rhetoric that penetrated intellectual, moral, and aesthetic values, this book owes much to the fact that modern literary theory has undermined the notion of the individual author and demonstrated the importance of context and convention to the existence of the text. The individual work simply becomes one articulation of a prevailing discourse. It is this discourse which is the ultimate object of the close reading of texts. The legitimacy of this kind of investigation depends on Michel Foucault's theory of discourse as explained in *The Order of Things*, even though this approach is not followed in a doctrinaire fashion. Recent works have demonstrated how Foucault's ideas can be applied to the study of literature and racial stereotyping: Edward Said's *Orientalism* and Christopher Miller's *Blank Darkness: Africanist Discourse in French*. Both books examine the use of stereotypes to keep the Orient and Africa respectively at a safe distance and, even more importantly, the capacity of these images to acquire a greater authority than reality itself.

Paul Fussell has shown in *The Great War and Modern Memory* that the imaginative persistence of a system of stark dichotomies dividing cultures makes the hope of synthesis impossible. There is no dialectic possible in a rigid system of images that emphasizes differences between 'We' on this side and the enemy over there. Literature for Fussell reveals how reality emerges as a moral landscape which is divided into known and unknown, safe and unsafe, clean and unclean. What is true of post-war European Literature is also evident in the way Americans depicted Haitians and vice versa. In the case of Haiti and the United States, literary representation allows insight into that manichean discourse, the binary vision of racial and cultural incompatibility used by both societies to define and defend themselves in the face of the other's disturbing presence.

J. M. D.

Acknowledgements

The present work grew out of research begun in 1983 in Washington, DC and Port-au-Prince, Haiti. The American part of the study was done at the Moorland-Spingarn Research Center of Howard University and the Library of Congress. During this time I was supported by a Senior Fulbright grant. I am grateful for the invaluable assistance of Jan Byrd of the CIES in Washington and Charlynn Spencer Pyne, Reference Librarian at the Moorland-Spingarn Center. I am also indebted to Mercer Cook, Brian Weinstein and Léon-Francois Hoffmann who always offered enthusiastic support. The Haitian part of the research could not have been accomplished without the patience and helpfulness of Frere Constant of St. Louis de Conzague as well as the encouragement of Roger Gaillard, Franck Etienne and Serge Garoute. Michel Fabre provided great assistance with the Black American reaction to Haiti and the librarians of the West Indies Collection of the Main Library of the UWI Mona were always supportive. A personal word of thanks to David Nicholls for his useful advice. My further thanks go to Sandra J. Deslandes who began typing the manuscript and to Marcia Lawrence and Valerie Gustaff who completed the job.

This book has taken four years to be conceived, researched and written. It was never intended as a virtuoso exercise in literary criticism. The original hope was that a study of this kind could, in its modest way, contribute to the demystification of the relationship between Haiti and the United States. This hope struggles to survive as the mythification of Haiti continues unabated.

Chronology

Year	Historical Event	Publications in the United States	Publications in Haiti
1776	Declaration of American Independence		
1779	Haitians join Americans in the Battle of Savannah		
1804	Haitian Independence		
1805		T. Branagan, *Avenia*	
1824	Emigration of American Freedmen to Haiti		
1825	France recognizes Haiti		
1852		H. B. Stowe, *Uncle Tom's Cabin*	
1855		W. W. Brown, *St. Domingo: Its Revolution and Its Patriots*	
1861	Redpath's promotion of Emigration to Haiti		
1862	America recognizes Haiti		
1873			D. Delorme, *Réflexions diverses sur Haiti*
1888		J. Whittier, *Anti-Slavery Poems*	
1889	F. Douglass and Mole St. Nicolas Affair		
1896			F. Marcelin, *Choses Haitiennes*
1907			J. N. Léger, *Haiti: son histoire et ses détracteurs*
1915	American Occupation		
1919	'Caco' rebellion and death of C. Péralte		
1920	J. W. Johnson visits Haiti for NAACP	E. O'Neill, *Emperor Jones*	*L'Union Patriotique* launched
1925		B. Niles, *Black Haiti*	
1929		W. Seabrook, *Magic Island*	D. Bellegarde, *L'Occupation Américaine d'Haiti*
1930	S. Vincent elected; Forbes Commission; Visit of Langston Hughes		L. H. Durand, *Trois Poèmes*; F. Burr-Reynaud, *Anathèmes*
1931	D. Bellegarde is Haiti's minister to the US; Walter White visits Haiti	F. Wirkus, *The White King of La Gonave*	

xiii

Chronology

Year	Historical Event	Publications in the United States	Publications in Haiti
1932		L. Hughes, *Popo and Fifina*	L. Laleau, *Le Choc*; *La Relève* launched
1933			S. Alexis, *Le Nègre masqué*
1934	Roosevelt's 'Good Neighbour' policy; End of Occupation	J. H. Craige, *Cannibal Cousins*	Haitian Communist Party, *Analyse schématique*
1935			M. Casséus, *Viejo*
1936	J. Roumain exiled after imprisonment		
1937		M. Herskovits, *Life in a Haitian Valley*	
1938		Z. N. Hurston, *Tell My Horse*	
1939	Roumain visits the US	A. Bontemps, *Drums at Dusk*; H. Courlander, *Haiti Singing*	J. Roumain, *Les griefs de l'homme noir*
1940			R. Piquion, *Un chant nouveau*
1941	E. Lescot elected; 'Campagne anti-superstitieuse' in Haiti		
1942	Creation of SHADA		
1943	US project to train Haitian teachers		
1944	Centre d'art opened; death of Roumain; A. Cesaire in Haiti	G. Myrdal, *An American Dilemma*	Roumain, *Gouverneurs de la rosée*
1945		J. Leyburn, *The Haitian People*	J. B. Cinéas, *L'héritage sacré*; R. Depestre, *Etincelles*
1946	A. Breton in Haiti; Lescot overthrown		
1947	Maya Deren in Haiti		
1949	E. Wilson in Haiti		
1957	F. Duvalier elected		Alexis, *Les arbres musiciens*
1959	Castro in Cuba denounces Duvalier		
1960	Depestre in Cuba		
1961	Alexis killed by army		
1963	Kennedy assassinated in the US; Duvalier denounces the US		E. Roumer, *Le caiman étoilé*
1964	Duvalier elected president for life; Relations with US resume		
1966		G. Greene, *The Comedians*	
1967			Depestre, *un arc-en-ciel l'occident chrétien*

Chronology

Year	Historical Event	Publications in the United States	Publications in Haiti
1970		Diederich and Burt, *Papa Doc*	
1971	Death of Duvalier and succession of Jean-Claude	R. Rotberg, *The Politics of Squalor*	
1972	Arrival of 'boat people' in Florida	I. Reed, *Mumbo Jumbo*	
1975			F. Etienne, *Dézafi*
1978		R. Heinl, *Written in Blood*	
1979	President Carter critical of Haitian Dictatorship. Jean-Claude allows political activity		Colimon, *Le chant des sirènes*
1980	US paroles illegal Haitian immigrants		J. C. Charles, *Le corps noir*
1986	Jean-Claude Duvalier leaves Haiti in a US Air Force jet	R. Banks, *Continental Drift*	

1
Through the Eyes of the Other: Stereotypes of the Nineteenth Century

PATRIARCHAL ATTITUDES

> Le noir me paraît être la race femme dans la famille humaine, comme le blanc est la race mâle.
>
> Gustave d'Eichtal, *Lettres sur la race noire*, 1839

'The Orient was almost a European invention' asserts Edward Said in his remarkable study of Western attitudes to the East (*Orientalism*, 1978). His provocative thesis is that Europe has produced a discourse, a rigid grid of stereotypes that allows a particular image of the Orient to filter into Western consciousness. These images of the East are neither simply picturesque nor innocent but an imaginative strategy which reinforces Western notions of superiority and defines the Orient as a commodity to be dominated or possessed. The idea of a geo-political awareness that is essentially imaginative provides a model for locating the element of mythification in relations between other countries. For instance, American attitudes to Haiti can be seen in terms of the creation of self-serving or rather self-aggrandizing images designed to tame the alien or threatening world on the outside. These images acquire a cumulative force over time and consistently resurface in order to define and reconstruct Haiti in terms which emphasize its difference or 'Otherness'.

Like the Orient, Haiti emerges as an inexhaustible symbol designed to satisfy material as well as psychological needs. Images of mystery, decadence, romance and adventure are not arbitrary in either case but constitute a special code, a system of antithetical values which establishes radical, ineradicable distinctions between the Subject and the Other, West and East, the United States and

Haiti. This systematic network of images eventually hardens into unshakeable dogma that is based on the notion of the 'Other' as the negative of the Subject, a zone of absence, a screen onto which the Subject projects his repressions. The 'Other' is denied its own subjectivity and simply exists so that the Subject can define itself. For instance Said's concern is to demonstrate that the Orient is fixed irrevocably in a prevailing discourse that privileges Western reason, lucidity and order over irrationality, mysticism and chaos. The 'Other' consequently is associated with a mentality, an atmosphere, a set of consistent characteristics which constitutes its essence.

An essentialist discourse derived from oppositions between light and dark, clean and unclean, good and evil can be identified in what Said terms 'textual attitudes'. In this regard Michel Foucault's concept of the world as a text is important. The word allows for a certain perceptive capacity, certain imaginative possibilities to exist. Stereotypes then form a kind of syntax, an orderliness that makes the world intelligible. The capacity of the word to reveal or delude is reflected in Foucault's assertion that 'Quixote reads the world in order to prove his books'.[1] The literary text describes, dramatizes and stabilizes the stereotypes that rationalize our view of the world. Indeed, the literary word can acquire a power greater than reality itself as we see in Quixote's quest for meaning in an alien and elusive universe. Thus flocks, inns and windmills become, because his imagination feeds on heroic images drawn from tales of romance and chivalry, armies, castles and knights. Imaginative literature must not be dismissed as self-indulgent fantasies or half-truths but should be seen as a repository for the organizing discourse that allows the Subject to perceive the 'Other' in a particular way. It is, perhaps, no accident that some writers, aware of the dangers of 'textualizing' the world, should create characters such as Emma Bovary and Don Quixote, who are tragically misled because what they have read makes it impossible to have an objective knowledge of the world around them.[2]

'Haiti was almost an invention of the United States' is a tempting version of Said's formulation. From the beginning, relations between Haiti and the United States were coloured by a tendency by the latter to project its fantasies and insecurities onto the recently independent black state. Haiti seems to have always had the lure of the extreme case, whether it was virgin terrain, a garden of earthly delights where the black race could begin again or the closest and most histrionic examples of Africa's continental darkness. These alternating stereotypes of a void to be filled or a flamboyant, inexcusable blackness constitute a binary model of differences that fixed the relationship between the United States and Haiti, between the diametrically opposed poles of mind and body, culture and nature, male and female. Haiti is imaginatively and culturally reconstructed as the 'Other', the negative or feminine and marginalized in a symbolic order devised by the United States. From the nineteenth century what beckons or revolts Americans is Haiti's impenetrable mystery, its irredeemable strangeness, its unpredictable 'Otherness'. Haitians are meant to be marvelled at, studied, converted, rehabilitated and ultimately controlled.

The constant scepticism that characterized American attitudes to Haiti in the nineteenth century is not unrelated to the way in which racialist thinking expressed itself at the time. In particular, the use of sexual polarizations to identify the differences between black and white, provides insight into the imaginative underpinning of stereotypes associated with Haiti. It has been shown that the single most influential work on racial theories in the nineteenth century Gobineau's *Essai sur l'inégalité des races humaines* (1853) consistently uses male and female metaphors to describe the hierarchy of races.[3] For instance the black and Jewish races are feminine as opposed to male whiteness. Gobineau's work represents a figurative and linguistic context for prevailing racialist rhetoric. Another example of this kind of sexual stereotyping of racial essence is apparent in the feminization of the Caribbean by metropolitan French writers from the eighteenth century. The well-known lament 'Adieu Foulards, Adieu Madras' celebrates the amorous helplessness of the Caribbean female at the point when her virile French lover is leaving her. The oppressive durability of these images of gentleness and dependency is quite remarkable and must be seen as the literary representation that defined the Caribbean in a posture of sexual surrender, awaiting the valorizing presence of the white, male colonizer.[4]

An English version of Gobineau's text was available in the United States as early as 1856 and entitled *The Moral and Intellectual Diversity of Races*. It could well have lent 'scientific' support to racial stereotyping in the United States in terms that emphasized the female dimension of blackness. The notorious benevolence of another influential nineteenth-century work Harriet Beecher Stowe's *Uncle Tom's Cabin* provides useful evidence of the 'textualizing' of the black race in the United States. In her novel the negro race is characterized by such virtues as 'simplicity of affection' and 'docility of heart'. She envisaged Africa as a 'far-off mystic land', a pastoral haven where this genius could flourish in an unhampered way. If allowed to develop according to its own peculiarities and limitations . . .

> The negro race, no longer despised and downtrodden will perhaps, show forth some of the latest and most significant revelations of humanlife. Certainly they will, in their gentleness, their lowly docility of heart, their aptitude to repose on a superior mind and rest on a higher power, their childlike simplicity of affection, and facility for forgiveness.[5]

It is difficult to imagine how this view of unprotesting submissiveness could be reconciled with the dramatic display of unrefined and violent behaviour exhibited during the Haitian war of Independence. The mulatto character George Harris does refer to Haiti but in dismissive terms. He theorizes that 'The race that formed the character of the Haytiens was a worn out, effeminate one'.[6]

Patriarchal condescension alternated with another sexual image of the volatile and unpredictable black race. The disarmingly earnest rhetoric of *Uncle Tom's Cabin* is often supplanted by images of a race prone to a lack of inhibition, self-control and restraint. In the same way that Gobineau believed in the sensual proclivity of the inferior races, blackness is the realm of passion for some American commentators in the nineteenth century. The fear of the power of this forbidden world and the need to exorcise this threatening dimension of delirium and anarchy is at the heart of the Rev. Josiah Priest's *Bible Defence of Slavery* (1851). In a discourse that fixes the black race in the realm of the corporeal, Priest focuses on the latter's suitability to physical labour – 'The extraordinary protrusion of the head', 'the leg nearly in the middle of the foot'.[7] Not submissively feminine by any means, the black race is to be dominated, shut away or excluded since 'The baleful fire of unchaste amour rages through the negro's blood'. Prone to hysteria and irresponsible behaviour, the black race could be subdued only by the confinement and supervision of slavery.

Whether the stereotype is benign or convulsive, supine or histrionic, the black race exists negatively. Its identity is reduced to the biological and seems fixed on the other edge of human culture. As a barrier against the turbulent, unknown world outside the black man is the frontier or border between known and unknown, order and chaos. Perhaps, because he is imaginatively situated on the edge, he can be ambiguously represented. He can either merge with the surrounding darkness as Josiah Priest's demonic version suggests or can be the shield that protects the world of order from the outer chaos. Whether virgin or whore, the black race's 'Otherness' is predetermined and 'textualized' by the middle of the nineteenth century. In confronting Haiti and the issue of a successful revolt of black slaves, the United States made use of the stereotypes that had been generated by its own experience of blackness. In order to deal with the disturbing and threatening existence of a state founded by ex-slaves, Americans resorted to the discourse that had already stabilized the way the black race would be perceived. Relations between the United States and Haiti were the political articulation of such a discourse and to this extent, it could be claimed that the United States almost invented Haiti imaginatively in the nineteenth century. Literary representations of Haiti are the key to the racial dichotomy that governs moral, aesthetic and intellectual views of Haiti. They do not emerge in a vacuum but reinforce and are in turn made more durable because of being tied to a particular set of political and economic circumstances.

The United States, the oldest republic in the Western Hemisphere, and Haiti, the first black republic, have strikingly similar origins. Historical parallels and continuities are inevitable since both countries gained their independence through a protracted war against a European power. A graphic illustration of shared political ideals can be seen in 1779 when over a thousand Haitian soldiers sailed from Cap Français with a contingent of French troops to fight with the Americans against British forces in the Battle of Savannah. Twelve years later the Haitian war of independence stimulated a demand for arms and ammunition which American merchants eagerly satisfied.

The impulse to celebrate the Haitian struggle for independence as an heroic and exemplary act is evident in the nineteenth century literary imagination. Writers such as Wordsworth, Lamartine and Victor Hugo all wrote idealistic tributes to Haitian independence and Toussaint Louverture in particular. There are traces of a similar shortlived idealism in the United States. For instance, the moral idealism and emotional rhetoric of Thomas Branagan's epic *Avenia: A Tragical Poem* (1805) is an American response to one of the great themes of Romantic Literature, the yearning for individual freedom. In Branagan's poem 'noble African citizens' fight under the inspired guidance of Toussaint to liberate themselves.

The sentimentalizing of the Haitian fight against slavery is also apparent in the verse of another abolitionist John Whittier in his *Anti-Slavery Poems, songs of labor and reform*. His poem to Toussaint Louverture treats the convulsive events in Haiti as an exemplary assertion of human rights. Toussaint is praised for his defiant fight against injustice. For Whittier, genetic or racial determinism are irrelevant to Haiti's example of a universal affirmation of the individual will.

> Dark Haytien! for the time shall come, yea,
> even now is nigh,
> When, everywhere, thy name shall be
> Redeemed from color's infamy . . .[8]

He goes to to emphasize the universal nature of the Haitian assertion of man's natural instinct to be free.

> In that strong majesty of soul
> which knows no color, tongue or clime,
> which still hath spurned the base control
> of tyrants through all time![9]

In this celebration of Toussaint's boldness and courage, Haitians are depicted as responsible and rational. However, the fear of slave insurrection ran deep in the white American imagination in the nineteenth century. Reports of carnage in St. Domingue; the arrival in 1793 of the first white refugees fleeing the war-torn 'French Island'; the restlessness among American slaves, when reports about the revolution in St. Domingue began to spread meant that the initial sympathy that existed among some would be swept away by the growing alarm in the United States over the potential for insurrection created by the Haitian example.

Haitian independence challenged the whole system of slavery and notions of black inferiority so violently that Rayford Logan, in commenting on its impact on the American consciousness, likens it to 'the effect that the Bolshevik revolution of 1917 produced upon the capitalistic nations'.[10] Fears of the influence of the successful slave revolt in St. Domingue on American blacks were not unjustified. Winthrop Jordan in commenting on precisely this phenomenon, notes that 'it is incontrovertibly evident . . . that a period of pronounced unrest among American slaves began not long after word arrived of racial turmoil in St. Domingo [sic]' and goes on to cite specific incidents of slave revolts inspired by the events on the 'French Island'.[11] Two reactions were forthcoming. Slave laws were reinforced to prevent the possibility for conspiracy or revolt and Haiti would have to be shut out or ostracized as an aberration.

Fear and distrust intensified the need for a discourse, radically different from the Romantic impulse earlier seen. In its mildest form, anxiety over the disruptive potential of Haiti's revolution, created a persistent reluctance among even the most progressive minds to recognize the parallels between Haiti and the United States. This can be seen in the ambivalence among those who believed in the ideal of revolution but could not bring themselves to accept the legitimacy of the newly independent black republic. Typical of this hesitation is Thomas Jefferson who had difficulty taking a positive stand on the Haitian question. His equivocation was provoked by an instinctive belief, on one hand, in the importance of revolution as an instrument of social change but his horror, on the other hand, at the prospect of slave rebellion. Consequently, he could never quite bring himself to condemn outright the right of the Haitian slaves to revolt nor give his approval. Instead, he rather gloomily predicted that Haiti would almost certainly spread the idea of rebellion to the United States. His later schemes of colonization for freed slaves stem from a desire to avert the carnage that would result from a vengeful black population. The deep disquiet created by the fear of a racial Apocalypse in the United States is present in his prediction of 'convulsions which would probably never end but in the extermination of one or the other race'.[12]

Jefferson's prevarication was relatively benign when compared to the open hostility displayed in some quarters. Jacques Léger in speculating about the 'origin of calumnies against Haiti' points to American sensitivity to the question of slave revolt as 'unquestionably the principal cause of the ill-will of the American people toward Haiti'.[13] By 'American people' he must have had in mind the Southern planters and their representatives in Congress. Their reactions seem provoked by a barely suppressed hysteria. There is no hint of the paralysing Northern Liberalism of Jefferson in their rejection of Haitian independence. They succeeded in effectively blocking recognition of Haiti for the first half of the nineteenth century. Haiti was recognized by France in 1825 and by Britain in 1833 in spite of the fact that neither country had officially abolished slavery at the time. They were both encouraged to grant recognition of Haitian independence because of the stability of President Boyer's regime that lasted 23 years (1820–43). American recognition came only after the secession of the South in 1862.

The ostracism of Haiti must also be seen in the light of American recognition of the former Spanish American colonies. In spite of their obvious instability, the United States began to recognize as early as 1822 the ex-colonies of Argentina, Chile and Mexico. The Southern planters, however, had their financial interests to protect and were particularly sensitive to the stereotypes of black restlessness and barbarity. Such fears are obvious in the case of Senator Benton of Missouri who, as Logan reports, argued that the United States should never . . .

> permit black consuls and ambassadors to establish themselves in our cities, and parade through the country, and give their fellow blacks in the United States proof in hand of the honors which await them for a successful revolt on their part.[14]

The stereotype of Haitian barbarity was highly favoured by those who believed that the sustained domestication of blacks was the only way of curbing their naturally barbarous instincts. Haiti then became the extreme example of blacks lapsing into savagery when restraints were lifted. The denial of recognition was the political manifestation of that discourse that denied the black race the right to subjectivity and relegated Haiti to a zone of negativity and absence.

This dogma based on antithetical values that made for racial incompatibility even permeated the anti-slavery movement in the United States. It is difficult to disagree with George Fredrickson's assertion that racialist belief in the nineteenth century was based on the idea of fixed, inherent characteristics of the various races. The hostility to Haiti can be seen as part of 'the tragic limitation of the white racial imagination of the nineteenth century, namely its characteristic inability to visualize an egalitarian biracial society'.[15] The anti-slavery movement, in spite of its laudable objective, could not bring itself to accept blacks as equals. The need to settle emancipated slaves outside the United States stemmed from the feeling that blacks and whites were racially incompatible and the fear, again articulated by Gobineau, that degeneration would result from racial mingling. On one hand, there was the belief that slavery was inhumane and could not be allowed to continue. Yet, it was felt that the freed slaves would have to be resettled elsewhere.

The beckoning void of Haiti was a tempting proposition for those who championed 'negro colonization'. Naturally, for some colonization was simply seen as an opportunity to deport troublesome freed slaves. But much more prevalent was the conviction that blacks were different and needed to develop on their own. The possibility of settling freed blacks in Haiti was first raised in the 1820s during the comparative peace of Boyer's presidency and later revived in the 1860s because of the imminence of emancipation and President Geffrard's receptiveness to this scheme. In Haiti, it was felt blacks could begin again and develop in an unhampered way as Harriet Beecher Stowe felt they should. Such perverse benevolence is evident in the statements of one of the most energetic promoters of 'Haytian Emigration' James Redpath. He promoted colonization in Haiti as an opportunity for American blacks to settle in 'a new Eden, in the most fertile of the Antilles'. Stowe's imagery is shared by the abolitionist Redpath who insisted that black Haitians were passive and without initiative . . . 'thoughtless of the morrow and without ambition'.[16] This vision of promissory emptiness again points to the feminine, supine stillness of Haiti.

Haiti could be used not only to solve the disturbing problem posed by the emancipation of American blacks but also to inculcate attitudes of restraint and sobriety. For instance, Maria Child, a white abolitionist, published in 1865 a guide to inspire young freedmen, entitled *The Freedmen's Book*.[17] Images of unprotesting passivity are pervasive in her singlemindedly genteel approach to the Haitian revolution. The violence of the latter is explained away as an aberration. The story of Toussaint dominates her carefully edited account of Haitian history. His is an exemplary life of intelligence, sobriety and industry which demonstrated the virtues of a religious upbringing. The figure of Toussaint, innocent and martyr, dominates her picture of Haiti. It is simply another example not of an objective truth but of the pervasiveness of one rhetorical strategy designed to keep Haiti at a distance. In its own way, it is no less pernicious than the Southern distrust of the barbaric unpredictability of the black mentality.

The prevalent literary representation of the black race as passive or comical, harmless entertainment in the nineteenth century, also indicates the imaginative constraints which would have impeded a fuller presentation of the events in Haiti. In his pretentious study of *The Negro Character in American Literature* (1926) John Nelson smugly observes that as far as the black character in fiction was concerned . . .

> his potential literary possibilities, at least such as made for buffoonery and humor, were clearly seen. As a mere comic character he was discovered. Unfortunately the same cannot be said for his discovery as a serious type.[18]

The nineteenth century insisted on seeing black characters in the roles of cook, gardener or maid and denied the possibility of seriousness by concentrating on peculiarities of speech, their fondness for music and their ability to dance. Sterling Brown remarks on the prevalence of the stereotype of the subdued black, dutifully reading his Bible in his cabin and concludes that 'The American reading public . . . accepted the delusion of the Negro as contented slave, entertaining child and docile ward'.[19] These images would only die when they were replaced in the early twentieth century by the flamboyance of the Harlem cabarets. From cabins to cabarets, from unprotesting docility to orgiastic revels the alternating stereotypes remain firmly intact. Haiti could not escape mythification within such a patriarchal value system that took as its main premise the otherness of the black race. An ineradicable discourse had fixed Haiti in the American imagination. This discourse would guarantee a constant stream of researchers, missionaries, adventurers and tourists with a taste for the outlandish. Haiti's predetermined strangeness, its strictly defined separateness had become the discourse that allowed it to be seen.

BLACK AMERICANS AND THE LURE OF SOLIDARITY

If the Haitian revolution was white America's nightmare, it fulfilled the most passionate dream of black Americans. The black American, himself stereotyped as the 'Other' in the United States, was unlikely to identify with the reductionist myths of Haiti's strangeness. He was more likely to see a war, successfully waged by black slaves against a European power, in admiring and idealistic terms. One of the earliest champions of the Haitian cause among black Americans was undoubtedly William Wells Brown. He wrote out of great feeling for, and actual personal experience of, Haiti. In a lecture delivered in 1854, some years after a visit to Haiti, Brown was effusive in his praise of Haiti's military leaders . . . 'No revolution ever turned up greater heroes than that of St. Domingo [sic]. But no historian has yet done them justice'. His was a fiercer view of the events in Haiti. The Southern fear of black excitability and the Northern hesitation over racial compatibility are not Brown's concerns. He presents a heroic picture of Haiti's revolutionary leaders:

Toussaint – 'his generosity, humanity and courage'
Christophe – 'a braver man never lived'
Dessalines – 'bold, turbulent and ferocious spirit'

Even if he tended to overstate his case and gloss over the difficulties of post-independence politics in Haiti, his effusion was not gratuitous but intended to present as dynamic and impressive an image as possible for his black American public. He was not so secretly hoping that the same scenario would be enacted in the United States.

> Who knows but that a Toussaint, a Christophe, a Rigaud, a Clervaux and a Dessalines may some day appear in the Southern States of this Union? That they are there, no one will doubt . . . and, if we are not mistaken, the day is not far distant when the revolution of St. Domingo will be reenacted in Southern Carolina or Louisiana.[20]

This is an early example of an enduring fascination with Haiti and with the figure of Toussaint in particular, among black writers and thinkers in the United States. For instance, the title of C. L. R.

James' study of the Haitian revolution *Black Jacobins* is further evidence of the power of early Haitian history over the imagination of black intellectuals in the West. Perhaps the praise showered on Toussaint is not unrelated to white Abolitionist approval of the latter as an exemplary figure. As a valiant martyr for the cause of black liberation, he became universally accepted as a model statesman for a racially embattled community. The close identification meant that he would be inevitably included in the various encyclopedia of black culture such as Brown's *The Rising Son* (1874). Another such anthology celebrating black chivalry and patriotism is Rev. Norman Wood's *The White side of a Black Subject* (1897). Toussaint features prominently in his Black Pantheon which includes Paul Dunbar and Frederick Douglass. These compilations of examples of racial achievement are meant to refute allegations of inferiority and irresponsibility. The Haitian revolution, not any more an example of unworthy and volatile black behaviour, was put forward as an example that blacks could be proud of.

Haiti as an independent nation of free black men continued to exert great influence on the imagination of American blacks in the nineteenth century. Early reports, such as those of Brown, emphasize the refinement of Haitian leaders, the pageantry of the court and Christophe's 'majestic bearing'. The possibility of migration to Haiti became a strong temptation as early as the 1920s. Loring Dewey, a member of the Colonization Society, seriously raised the possibility of settlement in Haiti as an alternative to African colonization. Dewey refers to Haiti's attractiveness to American blacks:

> Among the Coloured People themselves, a preference of Haiti over Africa was frequently expressed and among the whites . . . an assurance given of their ready aid to promote emigration to Haiti.[21]

In spite of the problems that divided Haiti and the United States at the time, the two republics seemed to agree on the issue of black migration to Haiti. From Jefferson to Lincoln there was clear approval of this scheme. Similarly in Haiti, this was seen as part of the mission of the first black republic and was explicitly encouraged by Boyer and Geffrard. Boyer, for example, responded to Dewey by claiming that it would give him joy to see . . . 'these scions of Africa, so abased in the United States, where they vegetate . . . transplanted to Haiti . . .'.²² Boyer also viewed the settlement of freed blacks in Haiti in more pragmatic terms. It could be a stimulant to economic prosperity and could also pave the way for eventual American recognition of Haiti. Yet this first effort was a dismal failure in spite of Boyer's good will and the attractions of Haiti to black Americans. In 1825 the majority of the migrants returned home. The scheme collapsed largely because there was difficulty in adjusting to Haiti in terms of language, climate or culture and they were certainly not prepared to adapt to Boyer's programme of agricultural development. Despite the eloquent tributes to the Haitian revolution, there were very real obstacles on the part of American blacks and, as we shall later see, on the part of some Haitians – to realizing concrete results from this vision of black solidarity.

Interest in 'Haytian Emigration' was renewed not long before the outbreak of the Civil War, when the abolitionist activist James Redpath was officially engaged by President Geffrard to promote this scheme among black Americans in 1861. His campaign was not without success and was supported by prominent members of the black community. Theodore Holly's series of articles entitled 'Thoughts on Hayti' appeared as early as 1859 proclaiming that the idea of migration to Haiti was divinely ordained.²³ In spite of Holly's highflown religious rhetoric, he is well informed on the Haitian political situation because of his visit in 1853. One of his articles is entitled 'The Disabilities under which the country labours' and it deplores the existence in the past of the dictatorships of Dessalines and Soulouque. He argues that Haiti needed 'The colored race in the United States . . .' who were in contact with 'a maturer and better developed civilisation than can be found in Haiti'. He was very aware of the failure of earlier efforts in this regard and warned against unrealistic expectations on the part of potential migrants from the United States.

Holly's articles not only mentioned the Haitian contribution to American Independence since Haitian troops 'fought side by side with American heroes in the battle of Savannah' but expressed the belief that Haiti 'holds the most important relation (to) the future destiny of the descendants of Africa'. Nevertheless, in spite of Holly's advice that only the 'choicest persons' should be selected for this venture, it was felt that the five thousand migrants did not represent the best elements of the black population. William

Wells Brown felt that the scheme could not attract 'the choicest persons' because '... men with stout hearts have no cause to emigrate'. What Brown does not mention is that the Civil War and the promise of emancipation made Haiti a less attractive proposition. In his biography of Brown, William Farrison makes this clear.

> ... by the end of 1861 it was becoming more and more evident that the Civil War would not be a brief, inconsequential episode ... and it was in the best interest of Negroes to remain in America.[24]

The recommendation that American blacks should stay and fight for abolition was also voiced by Frederick Douglass who had at one point favoured migration to Haiti. With the outbreak of Civil War in the United States, he declared that it was 'no time for us to leave the country'.

The dream of solidarity with the Haitian cause had been overtaken by events within the United States. After 1862 black Americans no longer saw migration as a priority but, in spite of a sentimental identification with the Haitian cause, began to see their racial destiny as separate from Haiti's. The episode of black migration to Haiti faded from the memories of both Americans and Haitians. Rulx Léon notes sadly that in Haiti '... memory of black American immigration is lost and the history books hardly mention it'.[25] 1862 also represents another phase in Haitian-American relations, it meant official recognition by the United States. By this time the latter had begun to emerge as a world power and her expansionist ambitions in the Caribbean made Haitians increasingly suspicious of American designs on Haiti. The major incident that marked this period of deep distrust is the attempt by the American government to acquire the Mole St. Nicolas as a naval station in 1889.

This episode is important to the sense of fraternity between black Americans and Haitians because of the involvement of the famous black abolitionist Frederick Douglass, whose role in this matter does demonstrate the intensity of the emotional ties between both black communities. Douglass was the American minister to Haiti at the time and was profoundly aware of the hostility that existed among members of his government to Haiti. He was later to criticize openly the rapacious nature of certain

American business interests and spoke with great passion about America's unjust involvement in Haiti's internal affairs. He referred to '. . . men in this country who, to accomplish their personal and selfish ends, will assist in setting revolutions afoot'.[26] Douglass' role was made even more complicated since his appointment was favoured by those who felt a black man was more likely to further the interests of the United States, since Haitians would not be suspicious of a prominent black who had fought against slavery.

However, in the negotiations to acquire a naval base at Mole St. Nicolas, Douglass, in spite of his role as official American representative, refused to be an accomplice to what amounted to a display of 'gunboat diplomacy'. He was very sensitive to national feeling among Haitians and was guided by the conviction that Haiti had '. . . no repugnance so deep seated and unconquerable as the repugnance to losing control over a single inch of her territory'. He was certainly seen as one of Haiti's more dependable friends in the United States and anticipated those prominent black Americans who came to Haiti's assistance during the American occupation.

THE OTHER AS SUBJECT: HAITIAN VIEWS OF THE UNITED STATES

He was part of my dream of course – but then I was part of his dream too!

Lewis Carroll

The closing lines of *Through the Looking Glass* provide a useful metaphor for understanding Haitian reactions to the United States in the nineteenth century in terms of parallel dreams. Just as the Red King is dreaming of Alice, who is in turn dreaming of the Red King, one can situate the attitudes of Americans to Haitians and vice versa as a series of reflections extending into infinity. Haitians had little sense of being looked at or dreamt by anyone else but had devised their own images, their own cultural code for dealing with their powerful neighbour to the North. Haiti protected its self-esteem by closely identifying with images of a refined, erudite and benevolent Europe. In contrast to the latter Americans were defined as being a coarse, immature and materialistic people.

Even if the prevalent tendency was to compare the United States unfavourably with Europe, the pragmatism associated with Anglo-Saxon culture did appeal to some Haitians. For instance, Henry Christophe in his rejection of French colonialism was decidedly pro-Anglo-Saxon in attitude. He not only insisted that his name be spelt with a 'y' but felt that English should be made the official language of his Northern Kingdom. This point of view never completely disappeared from the debate within Haiti on the orientation for the national culture. Many admired the achievements of a utilitarian and technological culture and the issue surfaced again in the campaign launched under President Nord Alexis (1902–8) to promote the merits of Anglo-Saxon pragmatism over irrelevant and backward 'latin' values.[27]

Nevertheless, it is true to say that in general Haitian attitudes to the United States were characterized by a certain uneasiness. The Mole St. Nicolas affair served to confirm Haitian suspicions and American plans were thwarted because of Haitian sensitivity to the idea of white foreigners on Haitian soil. Anténor Firmin, Haiti's foreign secretary at the time, simply refused to negotiate since any appearance of yielding to the United States in this matter would spell political disaster for his government. The United States may not have been a major concern of Haitian writers before the Occupation in 1915, but Firmin's refusal to compromise Haiti's independence is echoed by Haiti's staunchly nationalistic poets in the nineteenth century. For instance, Pierre Faubert was one of the first to warn his fellow citizens to put an end to political instability, since the United States, described as a rapacious vulture, had its eyes on Haiti. Haitians are exhorted to unite . . .

> Quand cette république, appui de l'esclavage,
> Rêve, avide, à vos champs fleuris!
>
> (When this republic, which supports slavery,
> greedily covets your flourishing fields)[28]

Faubert's fears were not unfounded and the threat of invasion or annexation grew steadily in the latter half of the nineteenth century. The possibility of annexation was even more disturbing because of growing instability within Haiti.

A constant theme of the anti-American sentiment in Haitian

writing is the frequent reference to the refinement and generosity of France. The Haitian élite, blindly eurocentric in their attitudes to taste, culture and social mores, rejected the United States as grasping and coarse. The stereotype of a humanitarian Europe always included references to writers and philosophers but never mentions Gobineau's influential work on racial differences or even Haiti's bitter struggle against France for independence. For instance, Faubert goes so far as to distort history when he claims that Europe approved of the Haitian revolution '. . . A nos braves/La vieille Europe applaudissait' (old Europe congratulated our brave men). Even those who were not as extreme as Faubert, consistently identified Haiti with the high-minded achievements of Europe. Damesvar Delorme writing in 1873 claimed that racial prejudice did not exist in Europe . . .

> L'Europe ne connait pas, elle, ces stupides et honteuses proscriptions de races.
> L'Europe de François Bacon, de Jean-Jacques Rousseau, de Vauvenargues, de Beccaris, de Schiller, de Lamartine, de Henri Brougham, n'admet de différence entre les hommes que celle que créent les aptitudes intellectuelles et les vertus.
> (Europe is free from these stupid and shameful racial prejudices.
> The Europe of Francis Bacon, of Jean-Jacques Rousseau, of Vauvenargues, of Beccaris, of Schiller, of Lamartine, of Henri Brougham sees differences between men only in intellectual calibre and moral virtue.)[29]

Similarly Frédérick Marcelin in his collection of essays entitled *Choses Haitiennes* (1896) refers to Haiti's spiritual and cultural affinity with France. He too is effusive in his praise for France's 'grandeur morale, générosité des sentiments, élévation des idées'.

The United States is stereotyped as the land of philistine extravagance and materialistic greed. This can be seen as an emotional strategy designed to reassure Haitians that in spite of their powerlessness, they were essentially superior to Americans. This self-serving rhetoric resurfaced consistently in the nineteenth century. In some instances the United States was not simply caricatured but a sneaking admiration for American achievement is expressed for the scale and the intensity of urban life. New York '. . . plus grand que Paris et plus luxueux. Les Américains ont la science, ils ont l'argent, ils ont l'orgueil'[30] writes Fernand Hibbert, who is overwhelmed by the marvels of Broadway, Fifth Avenue and Luna Park. For most Haitian writers, however, this is an alien, cluttered world. Even Hibbert deplores the fact that New York is living proof that money controls everything. Damesvar Delorme singles out the United States as the only example of rampant materialism in the world.

> Partout ailleurs, la civilisation signifie les efforts de l'humanité vers son amélioration morale, intellectuelle et physique tout à la fois; dans ce pays-là, civilisation signifie dollar, il s'agit uniquement de faire de l'argent; coûte que coûte.[31]

> (Elsewhere, civilization means humanity's striving equally for moral, intellectual and physical betterment; in that country, civilization means the dollar. It is simply a matter of making money at all costs.)

This systematic generalization of American culture as inhuman and destructive indicates the deep-seated distrust among Haitian intellectuals of technological progress. This issue would be the centre of bitter debates during the American Occupation. The intense nature of Haitian hostility to the United States is nowhere expressed more shrilly than in Massillon Coicou's poem 'Yankisme'. Coicou's fierce nationalism drives him to this tirade against American materialism, that bristles with anglicisms.

> Il faut de l'or – ou rien – pour être – ou ne pas être,
>   Time is money. Le crime aussi.
> Cotton is King! Ainsi, tandis qu'ils se réclament
>   De tant d'hommes au coeur si droit,
> Ainsi, comme l'Anglais, ces fiers yankees proclament
>   Que la Force prime le Droit . . .[32]

> (It is gold or nothing – to be or not to be
> Time is money. But so is crime.
> Cotton is King! So, while they boast of
>   So many stout-hearted men,
> So, like the English, these proud yankees proclaim
>   that Force is mightier than Justice)

The juxtaposition of English and French words, the contrasts between high-sounding phrases and unsavoury reality reveals the emotional charge behind the depiction of the American mentality. The strangeness of the United States had become a curiosity to be tirelessly catalogued and observed in the memoirs and travel books of Haiti's self-styled ethnologists. The former was depicted by Haitians as an objectionable moral landscape that would corroborate the perogatives they had ascribed to themselves.

If the United States was a zone of philistine excess it was also the land of the lynch mob. The persistence of racial prejudice in America was abhorrent to Haitian writers and they never stopped attacking this added feature of the sterility and inhumanity of American society. The only white American who seems to appear in a positive light in the Haitian literary imagination is, quite predictably, John Brown. The hanging of the white abolitionist in 1859 produced bitter reactions from Haiti's poets. For instance, Tertulien Guilbaud and Edmond Laforest treat in solemn and religious images the martyrdom of Brown. In both instances, he is compared to Christ who made the ultimate sacrifice for the love of his fellow men

> Le gibet du martyr fait songer à la croix![33]
> (The martyr's gibbet brings to mind the cross)
> Rédempteur des noirs, Brown meurt pour la liberté.
> Comme le Christ divin, rempli d'humanité.[34]
> (Redeemer of black men, Brown dies for liberty.
> Like the divine Christ, filled with humanity.)

The sublime, martyred figure of John Brown is celebrated in order to remind Haitians of the brutality of their Northern neighbour. Haitians were also warned with growing frequency of the terrible consequences of having so prejudiced a state intervene in Haiti's internal politics. Delorme sounds this note of alarm when he predicts that if the Americans annexed or occupied Haiti, Haitians . . .

> vous serez maintenus dans une sujetion aussi dure que l'esclavage. . . . On vous méprisera, on vous maltraitera, comme on méprise et maltraite les hommes de notre race aux Etats-Unis.[35]

(You will be maintained in a state of submission as painful as that of slavery. . . . You will be scorned, treated badly, just as men of our race are scorned and treated badly in the United States.)

The fear of returning to a state of slavery, this time with American masters, provoked a shudder of revulsion among Haitians. In an effort to demonstrate just how badly blacks were treated in the United States, Haitian commentators at the time set out to show how degraded and unprotesting the American black had become. One of the earliest recorded reactions to black Americans can be found in Ardouin's description of black freedmen who had resettled in Haiti under Boyer. They appear to be spectres of humiliation and defeat. Their pitiful appearance is established through such details as their battered trunks, their old suitcases, their woollen rags.[36] Ludicrous and deformed, they were kept at a distance, morally and culturally, by Haitians who regarded themselves as superior because they were no longer enslaved. The persistence of this negative stereotype of black Americans has been noted quite often. Emily Balch in reporting on the American Occupation in 1927 was moved to observe that there 'seems to have been a tendency for Haitians to look down on American negroes, whose slavery is more recent'.[37]

Among some writers at the turn of the century this attitude sometimes degerated into a smug and supercilious posture. For example, Frederick Marcelin who is so passionate in his defence of Haiti against Haitians being caricatured as 'des sauvages et des grotesques',[38] is guilty of precisely the same thing when he speculates that 'le type du colored people' were inferior. In his memoirs *Au gré du souvenir* he contrasts the proud Haitian with the humiliated American.

> Le type haitien est non seulement plus affiné, mais il a plus de fierté, plus d'aisance dans les manières et dans l'allure. . . . Le noir américain baisse la tête et ses yeux semblent toujours regarder le sol.[39]
>
> (The Haitian type is not only more refined, but he is more proud, more confident in his manner and comportment. , The black American has his head lowered and his eyes seem always fixed on the ground)

Fernaud Hibbert's protagonist in *Le manuscrit de mon ami* makes similar observations about differences between the black race in Haiti and the United States.

Tous ceux que j'ai rencontrés sont laids, – les hommes comme les femmes. Le type n'est pas fin et gracieux comme chez nous.[40]

(All those I have met are ugly – men as well as women. The type is not refined and graceful as in our land.)

Similarly, Delorme in his sharp critique of American society in *Réflexions diverses sur Haiti* describes his horror at witnessing an example of racial prejudice in the streets of New York and declares that the most humble Haitian would not have submitted to such treatment. Blacks in the United States he laments are forced to live like Jews in the Middle Ages, tolerated but persecuted.[41]

In the nineteenth century Haitians shut themselves up in a world of gentility, elegance and Old World nostalgia. From this imaginary, patrician haven they superciliously regarded the world around them as barbaric and unformed.[42] Contemptuous of material progress and technological achievement, they prided themselves on their fastidious and noble seclusion. Haiti could be said to have invented itself in the nineteenth century by insisting on self-regarding images of a land isolated in time and space. Some were becoming worried about 'une légende malveillante' made up of 'racontars de journaux, les récits fantastiques de voyageurs'[43] which painted a lurid and sensationalist picture of Haiti as a land of cannibalism and anarchy. For the most part, however, they had little sense of being looked at. The world was part of the dream of these New World 'hidalgos'. Shabby but clinging desperately to the splendour of their past, they made their Quixotesque journey through the nineteenth century hopelessly disoriented because their outdated codes had unfortunately acquired a greater authority than lived experience. In the early twentieth century Haiti would have to face the consequences of this tragic disparity between the stubbornly unyielding nature of reality and an imaginative discourse that was incapable of generating reliable images.

2
Through the Looking Glass: Textual Politics and the American Occupation

THROUGH A GLASS DARKLY

> Ah! te voilà Voix Blanche. . . . Tu es la voix des forts contre les faibles
>
> L.-S. Senghor, *Chaka*

The military intervention of the United States in Haitian affairs in 1915 initiated an intense and bitter phase in relations between the two republics. Perhaps even more decisively than the numerous political commentaries of the time, the fiction and travel books of the period reveal the unofficial truth of the Occupation. Often the literature of this period in a shrill and explicit fashion returned to many of the stereotypes that had evolved during the preceding century.

The majority of American commentators on Haiti during the Occupation can be likened to Alice when she enters that strange, illogical other world in *Through the Looking Glass*. These travel books or thinly-disguised autobiographies all singlemindedly focus on what Lewis Carroll called 'the effect of living backwards' in their accounts of exotic ritual or barbaric sacrifice in the Haitian countryside. Whether they were aware of it or not, these books had much to do with justifying America's 'civilizing mission' in Haiti at the time. They provided images that were ultimately cherished as the rationale for America's imperialist designs on Haiti. Lurid accounts of savagery and cannibalism could not, perhaps, in themselves dictate national policy but under pressure of national and strategic interests they did reinforce the feelings that American intervention in Haiti was the only way of curbing that nation's barbarous instincts.

The feeling that unrestrained blacks would lapse into savagery was a pervasive one in the nineteenth century and effectively blocked the United States' recognition of Haiti until 1862. These ideas never disappeared and acquired a new currency after the events of 1915. However, even before this time it is clear that certain stereotypes of Haiti had become firmly fixed in the American imagination. For instance, Frederick Douglass felt the need in 1983 to defend Haiti against the prejudices of 'newspaper correspondents and six day tourists' by pointing to the fact that Haiti seemed capable of enduring prolonged crises without '. . . falling to pieces and without being hopelessly abandoned to barbarism'.[1] Nevertheless, a school of sensationalist journalism had already begun to emerge and it certainly fed its insatiable reading public some of the wildest fantasies it could concoct. This cannot be seen as an entirely innocent exercise since it ultimately recommended that the United States immediately put a stop to this irresponsible and barbaric behaviour in a neighbouring republic. A perfect example of the kind of prejudiced commentator that Douglass was reacting against is Frederick Ober. In his travel book *In the Wake of Columbus* (1893) he insists on the widespread practice of cannibalism in Haiti and on the duty of the United States to save Haiti from a further decline into barbarism:

> The Black Republic cannot endure another century as it is going now, without calling to it the attention of the world, and exciting its strongest reprobation. It is the desire of more than one government that the United States should take this irresponsible island republic in hand and administer to it a salutary lesson.[2]

Consistently the various commentators of the time return to the question of cannibalistic practices and the need for the United States to intervene in the lives of what the journalist and publisher William Boyce called 'these happy-go-lucky children of nature'. He also hinges his argument for Haiti's uncivilized behaviour on 'this horrible form of sorcery with its cannibalistic rites' which he admits 'has long been a headliner in the newspapers'.[3]

The dismayingly simplistic views of these turn-of-the-century commentators do have an interesting literary origin. Spenser St.

John's lurid *Hayti or the Black Republic*, which is actually quoted by Ober, launched a school of sensationalist journalism in the nineteenth century that had created an enthusiastic following among American journalists and travel writers. 'The Black Republic' as St. John called it, inspired the same shudder of disgust among his successors as it did in the Victorian imagination. Ludwell Montague is aware of this phenomenon in Haitian/American relations as he points out in his *Haiti and the United States* (1714–1938):

> St. John ... revealed to the world the journalistic virtues of voodoo. His *Hayti or the Black Republic* has had a numerous progeny, even to the present day, works of which the inspiration is obvious, with or without due acknowledgement.[4]

The numerous progeny inspired by St. John's book were never more in evidence than during the American Occupation. Interestingly, these adventures in a parallel universe did not always share the same attitudes to Haiti. Their views ranged from the smug and patronizing to a wide-eyed, negrophile enthusiasm for the strange values and practices of the Haitian folk. What they held in common was the conviction that Haiti was different from the rest of the world. Consequently, although they might differ on the nature of this difference, they shared a taste for the theatrical and the melodramatic that ensured their commercial appeal. They all, in varying degrees of shrillness, cultivated a style based on hyperbole and sensationalism, which owed much to that earlier imaginative rhetoric that facilitated attitudes of domination and distrust. The clearest example of this strident and melodramatic tone is to be found in the work of John Houston Craige whose very titles betray the hostile intent of his books – *Cannibal Cousins*[5] and *Black Baghdad*.[6] In a text largely constructed from dramatic anecdote and smug digressions on the question of racial inferiority, Craige is hypersensitive to the 'sinister suggestions of menace' that seem ubiquitous in the Haitian countryside. The incidents in his narrative are accompanied by a bizarre sound track composed from 'the syncopated thump of innumerable tom-toms ... blended with the shrill piping of bloodthirsty malaria mosquitoes'.

In Craige's world even the mosquitoes are touched by that cannibalistic impulse which is pervasive in that sinister, mysterious world. What is more complex is the case of those writers who entered this 'looking-glass world' not seeking high moral ground from which to criticize what they saw but rather willing to celebrate the marvellous strangeness of Haitian culture in the face of the inhibitions of Western civilization. For instance, the decidedly negrophile works of William Seabrook and Blair Niles are effusive accounts of the richness of Haiti's folk culture with its access to that 'secret vital world' lost to the West. Yet it should be noted that these admiring tales of Haiti's folk heritage were in their own indirect and well-meaning way akin to the colonizing impulse we find in Houston Craige. Niles and Seabrook are no less one-sided in their depiction of the mysteries of the Haitian interior. However, unctuous racial arrogance has been replaced by an imaginative plundering of Haiti for the fatigued West – essentially an intellectual 'nostalgie de la boue'.

Consequently, we can divide American commentators into two broad categories: apologists for the Occupation and defenders of negro primitivism. In the former Craige and Faustin Wirkus are worthy of close scrutiny. In the latter, Seabrook and Niles are the two most vocal exponents of the virtues of Haiti's black soul. Naturally these texts do not exhaust the variations in American reaction to Haiti at the time. For example, the little-known novel *Knights of the Cockpit* (1931) in which a squadron of Marine pilots do battle with Haitian guerrillas trained by the Germans in the use of machine guns, is easily one of the most far-fetched tales to emerge from the Occupation. It owes more to the tales of Rider Haggard than to the realities of 'caco' resistance against the Marines. Similarly, Edna Taft's *A Puritan in Voodoo-land* (1938) is a sustained 'frisson' of fear and trepidation on the part of a sensitive and vulnerable American female who finds herself plunged into a disorienting milieu of dark, menacing hills and the 'savage rhythms of vodoo drums'. The aggressively uneven terrain is overemphasized so as to demonstrate Haiti's volatile ethnic reality. Overwhelmed by this strange, primeval world, our prim narrator laments the fact that the American invasion is unappreciated by Haitians.

Interestingly, the only real departure from the eccentricities of this period is an unpublished work by the naval officer Edward Beach which he optimistically entitled *The Last Haitian Revolution*. It was perhaps too reasonable a view of Haiti to meet with commercial success. Beach was evidently quite irritated by the tradition of damaging and sensationalist reporting on Haiti. His observation on this question is perhaps a comment on the fate of his own unpublished manuscript which did not contain that element of wild fantasy that guaranteed publication and an enthusiastic readership for many other less informed and less accurate accounts.

> Haiti has been cursed by the visitor of a few days who collects tales of poisoning, snake worship, voodooism and cannibalism, and writes with self assumed authority, for newspapers and magazines articles that must be highly colored to secure publication.

Beach's feelings in this regard are echoed in his novel which contains one protagonist who is seen as typical of the timid, uninformed creature who is capable of recounting the most macabre tales about Haiti. Mr. Hammond, an ageing, small-town school teacher, is sent to Haiti to do a series of articles. His mind is made up even before arriving that this was a country 'of African savages, a country of violent revolution, anarchy, assassination, cannibalism, poisoning, everything horrible'.[7] His behaviour in Haiti is a strong satire of that of the frightened foreigner who is too afraid to expose himself to the world around him and reinforces his own prejudices through second-hand sources.

> So convinced was he of the dangers that surrounded him that, except in company of foreign residents he met, he never left the hotel. These foreigners were amused at his fears and told stories that increased them and as he believed every yarn told him he was given a hash of horrors seldom heard anywhere, even in Haiti.[8]

Beach's novel sets out to give a balanced account of the events that led to the landing of American Marines in 1915. It is very much a 'roman à clef' in which the unscrupulous president Santerre is Guillaume Sam and the mob violence of 1915 is explained in political and human terms and not as a nation succumbing to atavistic urges. His text even contains Haitian protagonists who speak lucidly about Haiti's evolution and the possibility of future regeneration. The final chapter 'Phoenix Rises from the Ashes' is naively confident in detailing the achievements of the Occupation. Beach does not hesitate on the question of the legitimacy of the American presence on foreign soil yet his general attitude is refreshingly benign. For once the Occupation is not presented by an American officer as a salutary lesson nor are Haitians seen as pathetic children.

The offerings of Craige and Wirkus, however, are unrelenting in their effort not only to justify the Occupation but to paint an outrageously racialist picture of Haitian society. The tone of both these commentators is arrogant and they both set out to fix a pathetic and absurd image of Haiti after which they enjoy the luxury of being superior and patronizing. For instance, they are irritatingly consistent in their depiction of characteristics of the Haitian personality. For Craige there seem to be only two types of Haitians: either the untamed savage or the docile and obsequious domestic. His orderly is unprotestingly subservient '. . . good-natured, humorous and true as steel'. In *Black Baghdad*, which unites images of Eastern decadence and black savagery, the stereotype recurs in the figure of his 'boy' who is described as 'a simple soul'. The simple-minded self-assurance of Wirkus encourages him to be even more expansive in this regard. Haiti was 'the gateway to a world of jumbled savagery—childlike lovableness and faith'.[9] In his memoir *The White King of La Gonave*, Haitians were 'always singing, improvising songs like happy children' and blacks as a whole were 'more nearly children than whites'. In their minds there is only one other variation on the Haitian character. The image of the volatile, unpredictable black is invoked to demonstrate the 'brute throwback to jungle ancestry'. Invariably the figure of the irrational Haitian who has gone monstrously berserk turns up '. . . Nostrils dilated, lips drawn back over his strong white teeth, enameled eye balls projecting far out of his head . . .'. It is also clear that these stereotypes echo the images of blacks favoured by the ante-bellum South. The Occupation seems to present the opportunity for reliving the paternalist myth of the Southern plantation. Neither Craige, who describes himself as an 'honest imperialist', nor 'the white king of La Gonave' really detain themselves with the official objectives of the Occupation. Craige is quite frank about what he sees as the lack of potential in Haiti for developing democratic structures. In *Black Baghdad* he claims . . .

> These people had never heard of democracy and couldn't have comprehended it had they heard. They had been ruled by

despots, and despotism was the only government they could understand.

(p. 15)

Wirkus' ideas on the subject verge on the ludicrous as he offers his own speculations about how the 'primitive' Haitian mind viewed the presence of the Marines – 'we were sent to spank them as agents of an angry god or we came to protect them from new tyranny as the agents of a god'. Whatever their role – punitive or paternalist – their status was never in doubt. It is difficult to imagine such men as the enlightened instruments of civilization. Their role was to 'pacify' or 'deliver a salutary lesson'. It is not hard to see why American officers are shown as brutish and vulgar in Haitian writing at the time. However, what they revealed in their own accounts of the Occupation far surpass even the most bitter Haitian satire of the American officer.

As far as both Wirkus and Craige were concerned, the only good Haitian was a servile one. In fact they both subscribed to the notion of creating in Haiti a replica of the harmony and efficiency of the ante-bellum Southern plantation. Craige is unequivocal in his conclusion about the Haitian need for authority and control. There seemed to be something in the Haitian mentality that '. . . renders it almost impossible for him to resist a forcible command . . . submissiveness is ingrained in their race'. Wirkus also clings to this fantasy. It is difficult to imagine that he is referring to the use of peasant work-gangs under the *corvée* law. The conditions under which Haitians were forced to work, were considered by many observers to be intolerable. James Weldon Johnson talked about Haitians 'beaten into submission', about 'long hours of unremitting labor' in describing the brutal application of the *corvée* law. However, Wirkus enthuses at seeing gangs of black workers toiling happily under the sun.

> It was a delight to go through the long stretches of road under construction by gangs of a thousand to fifteen hundred men working together.
> The Haitian works best as a member of a team. The larger the team the more efficient the individual. . . . They would keep this up all day as they swung in time to the cadence of the picks.

(p. 191)

Both apologists for the Occupation alternate in their narratives between bizarre anecdotes and wild digressions on the question of race and culture. The latter tend to be both pretentious and anti-intellectual at the same time. Their view of the world was singlemindedly manichean and they had no time for liberal attempts at cultural relativism. Wirkus is for instance very snide on the subject of intellectuals with humanitarian scruples. He talks about being at a party of 'advanced thinkers' and 'social idealists' in Greenwich Village and mockingly compares their earnestness to that of 'the dancers and drinkers of a Haitian backwoods "bamboche" '. Craige likewise issues a warning to those with scruples on the question of race. He speaks of an American officer with reservations about the Occupation, who was captured and eaten by Haitian bandits. The moral of this tale is loudly proclaimed '. . . do not ever doubt your superiority over these people'. Any other attitude is seen as naively highbrow.

These accounts of Marines' experiences in Haiti are also filled with the most expansive grandiloquence on the onward march of the white race and civilization. Haiti and the fate of 'these people' to them were part of a larger scenario in which the 'civilized world' was rightfully asserting itself against the weaker inferior races. A crudely manipulated Darwinism is ever present in this justification for American expansionism. Once again the question of race profoundly determined attitudes to Haiti and had much to do with the shaping of national policy. Craige sanctimoniously pronounces Haiti part of a global pattern of the inevitable assertion of racial superiority.

> . . . just as the white man's law, the white man's religion were all the while marching on to dominate and change the strange primitive life that played about them. . . . The new against the old; the complex against the simple; the sophisticated against the primitive. The old story. The story of Hinche. The story of Haiti. The story of the world.
>
> (p. 37)

Their sense of racial superiority is so intact that it never seems to occur to them that these remarks may in any way be offensive or indeed harm the objectives of the cause they were serving. We see again a vulgar application of cultural Darwinism in that their feelings of racial superiority are explained in terms of a higher law of nature which dictated that it was inevitable that superior races should dominate inferior ones. This is presented as the natural order of things that liberalism naively violated. It is in fact difficult to see how the stated objectives of the Occupation could be achieved given this sense of cultural antithesis among those who played a prominent role in Haiti during those nineteen years.

To the same extent that Haiti was perceived as a land of timeless barbarity by Craige and Wirkus, it had become a zone of seductive and unrestrained sensuality to many travel writers in the 1920s. The latter also shared the notion that race determined culture but unlike our Marine commentators, they did not see Haiti as degraded but as a primitive Eden. At this time travel books specialized in ecstatic and sensational accounts of journeys to 'primitive' regions. For instance *Black Laughter* (1924) and *Ebony and Ivory* (1925) by Llewelyn Powys which contain lurid tales of Africa, or *Tom-tom* by John Vandercook which treated the bush-negroes of Surinam. Scenes of joyous abandon abound in these accounts of the uninhibited and energetic animality of 'primitive' peoples. There is no impulse to reform or alter these savage worlds. On the contrary such a view is supplanted by a fiercely Rousseauesque defence of black cultural authenticity, of an Eden magically arrested before the Fall. This prelapsarian nostalgia has its origin in the stereotypes of national and racial genius that earlier provoked attempts at colonization of freed blacks outside of the United States. This ecstatic negrophilia was based on notions of 'primitive' behaviour that were intact in these wonderfully different societies. Indeed the larger intent behind these texts was to demonstrate the difficulty of racial miscegenation and the need to keep races 'pure'. The reviewer of Vandercook's *Tom-tom* highlights this argument and quotes the author's words in *Opportunity*:

> To my mind there is no hope for the modern negro in the way he is now vainly going. Slavery lasted too long and ended too suddenly for the white ever to forget and forgive enough to allow black people into our sancta.[10]

Black nationalism has had some curious adherents in its time.

It is not surprising that Haiti should be included among those countries which were culturally distinct. Haiti's reputation in this regard was assured since the nineteenth century. One exasperated reviewer in *The Crisis* laments in 1935 . . .

> There seems to be a rule that requires travelers to Haiti to offer for the palate of sedentary readers as gruesome and weird a picture as possible of voodoo practices and beliefs. . . . There has been far too much play upon the barbaric and the weird in dealing with things Haitian. A common sense attitude with a sound scientific approach is a crying need.[11]

Already help was on the way in that informed anthropologists had begun working on scientific descriptions of Haitian society.[12] But for the moment the mood was one of sustained fantasy – Haiti as spectacle, as sensory experience. Two of the most characteristic and most widely read of these travel books are: *Black Haiti: A Biography of Africa's Oldest Daughter* by Blair Niles and *The Magic Island* by William Seabrook. Anti-materialist and negrophile in outlook, both Niles and Seabrook unequivocally defended Haiti's right to develop (or not develop) according to the dictates of its own folk soul. They consequently disagreed with the Occupation since it put an end, according to Seabrook '. . . to the freedom of a negro people to govern or misgovern themselves'. Blair Niles also romanticizes Haiti's right to a primitive soul. She is at her most effusive when she declares:

> Haiti has a song in its heart; and no matter how desirable the gifts we bring, they are worthless in comparison: it is all important that Americanization should stop with order and science; it must not stifle the song in hearts that yet remember how to set life to music.[13]

It is not that there was not in theory some reason behind this fear of the corrosive effect of materialism. However, neither writer seemed to notice that the benefits of modern civilization were not being brought to Haiti. In fact, their fear that Haiti might become culturally contaminated far outweighed any apparent concern with either the nature of Haiti's problems or how they could be solved. Ultimately this vision of unrestrained sensuality and bountiful nature simply glossed over the real tragedy of the Haitian situation.

These travel writers may have avoided the vision of racial

Apocalypse, highly favoured by their contemporaries in the Marines, but their own brand of romantic racialism ultimately created the impression of almost childish irresponsibility in their accounts of Haiti. Niles in the subtitle to her book – 'Africa's Oldest Daughter' – conveys the impression of supine, unprotesting sensuality. Images of fragility, of a graceful impotence replace the inhospitable and sinister world of Craige and Wirkus. Niles regrets what she sees as 'the gradual evolution of peasant and primitive peoples' without reflecting on the intensity of the tragedy that lay below the surface of these quaint worlds. Seabrook is no less insistent on the existence of a kind of primal innocence among Haitians.

> The Haitian peasants are thus double natured in reality – sometimes moved by savage, atavistic forces whose dark depths no white psychology can ever plumb – but often, even in their weirdest customs, naive, simple harmless children.[14]

The danger of presenting Haitians as just so many writhing, naked bodies is very slyly referred to by Jean Price-Mars in his reaction in 1929 to Niles' *Black Haiti*. In his view the Occupation becomes an inevitable form of 'purdah' inflicted on 'Africa's oldest daughter' because of her misconduct. The sinister effect of the 'feminisation of Haiti' had become apparent.

> . . . un beau jour, la pauvre fille est accusée de manquer à la morale, de gaspiller ses ressources, et de nuire à la sécurité des voisins. Au nom de l'ordre elle est traduite par-devant qui de droit et prestement mise sous tutelle.[15]
>
> (. . . one fine day, the poor girl is accused of lacking in morality, of squandering her gifts, and endangering the security of her neighbours. In the name of discipline she is brought before the proper authorities and quickly placed under supervision)

In their reaction against American Puritanism, and a sense of the Western World's enslavement to materialism, Niles and Seabrook concentrated on the expressiveness and spontaneity of the Haitian folk and were sharply critical of the élite for not recognizing the validity of Haiti's African soul. In this respect they were simply part of the chorus of protest against the élite that emanated from

the Haitians themselves[16] but, even if some of this hostility to the
élite was justified, they seemed unaware of the severe limitations
of their own prescriptions for cultural authenticity. It would
almost seem that there was some consensus on this question of
the excessive westernization of the mulatto élite. John Vandercook,
himself a travel writer, in 1927 accused the Haitian élite of having
'gone white too desperately'.

> And the ruling classes . . . have implicitly accepted the
> essentially American premise that the white race and white
> civilization are the best, the last and the ultimate perfections of
> evolutionary destiny. It is rather troubling to see where the
> logical development of that idea has led them.[17]

The criticism of America's high-minded, reformist zeal is refreshing
but the blanket condemnation of the élite in the name of racial
authenticity is itself an aberration. Unfortunately this romantic
racialism also insists on temperamental differences between races –
this time the hierarchy is inverted since the colourful and spirited
black is seen as superior to the bland, inhibited white. This would
seem to be a benign twist to a stereotype launched in Rev. Josiah
Priest's *Bible Defence of Slavery* (1825) in which the sexually
uninhibited black burns with 'the baleful fire of unchaste amour'.

It is in this spirit that Niles attacks the élite for abandoning the
'virtues of the race', and ignoring 'the great gifts which their race
might make to a drab and waiting world; gifts of rhythm and of
imagery and of joy'. Seabrook is equally insistent on presenting
the élite as a soulless, repressed group uncomfortable in their
world of artificial sophistication '. . . shut behind the fashionable
convent culture, the Paris gowned sophistication, the facile small
talk'. The Haitians who meet with their approval are almost
startlingly physical and muscular '. . . leaping, screaming,
writhing black bodies' or 'young muscular . . . slenderwaisted,
with broad shoulders, barefooted'. Niles offers an image of a
people without affectation or inhibition who contributed to 'the
sensuous undulating dance of life under tropic stars'. In both
writers this rhapsodic impulse lurks always ready to criticize the
loss of a sense of mystery in the West and to celebrate the
emotional intensity of the underdeveloped world. Seabrook in
one of his moments of effusion suggests the real origins of this
obsession with sensuality. Haiti was clearly a victim of the blind

quest for primitivism in the 1920s. *The Magic Island* was meant to bring vicarious satisfaction to those who sought this kind of novelty and disorientation in the nightclubs of Harlem at the time.

> It was savage and abandoned, but it seemed to me magnificent and not devoid of a certain beauty. Something inside me awoke and responded to it. . . . Of what use is any life without its emotional moments or hours of ecstasy? . . . What, after all, were they doing here in these final scenes . . . that was so different from things which occur in our own fashionable and expensive night clubs, except that they were doing it with the sanction of their gods.
>
> (pp. 42–3)

In this need to liberate man's unconscious forces, the world of urbane respectability of the Haitian élite did not stand a chance.

The vision of Haitian 'joie de vivre' that pervades *Black Haiti* and *The Magic Island* has its roots in notions of blackness that were fashionable in the 1920s. In the wake of a growing disenchantment with the confining values of Puritanism, post-war America turned to the negro as a creature whose life was not cramped by a strict moral code – an example of the unfettered, elemental ideal. This is the time when Harlem was in vogue. But for those who wished to reach beyond the exotica of Harlem, Haiti became the accessible and authentic next stop in the quest for a world of primal innocence. The parallels between Harlem and Haiti were underlined by the French journalist Paul Morand who felt that if Harlem were left to develop on its own it 'would quickly revert to a Haiti, given over to vodoo'.[18] Furthermore Haiti could offer all the thrills of an African safari with little or no risk since the Marines had already done their job of 'pacification'. It is therefore not surprising that these travel writers should be so insistent on throbbing drums and gyrating bodies and so neglectful of the more mundane aspects of daily life in Haiti. Their public avidly sought images of sensuality and abandon that surpassed what could be found in the cabarets of Harlem. Indeed Haiti was a more authentic Harlem, valued for its earthiness and sensuality.

The 1920s mark the transition from the modest, subservient world of *Uncle Tom's Cabin* to the wild exuberance of the nightclubs of Van Vechten's *Nigger Heaven*. The criteria for black acceptability had been radically redefined. The image of timidness and docility advocated by Harriet Beecher Stowe was woefully inadequate at this time when the Protestant virtues of austerity and self-denial were replaced by a compulsive struggle on the part of post-war America to liberate the individual unconscious. The urgency of this need quickly promoted among many white intellectuals and sophisticates an interest in and dependence on the negro as an example of someone who had been mercifully spared the drab, civilizing virtues of Western culture. The chaotic, impulsive world of the primitive was located in Harlem where as Sterling Brown observes '. . . what emerges is a Negro synchronized to a savage rhythm, living a life of ecstasy'.[19] The individual who most successfully promoted this vogue of the primitive was Carl Van Vechten who epitomized the longings and fantasies of this generation. His novel *Nigger Heaven* (1926) is notorious for its fascination with the exotic black underworld of Harlem and the kind of stylistic exuberance that is characteristic of Seabrook's evocation of jungle orgies in Haiti. In describing the aim of this novel, Nathan Huggins shows the extent to which it clearly anticipates the arguments of Niles and Seabrook '. . . Indeed, the novel seems to argue that the Negro 'civilizes' himself at great cost'.[20] It is interesting to note the extent to which some of these notions were adopted by black writers at the time. The latter seemed equally capable of seeing Haiti and Harlem through 'white' eyes. This tendency would be discredited only in the late 1930s and 1940s when this vision of black 'joie de vivre' is replaced by proletarian violence.

Perhaps the one positive element in all this is the promotion of black themes as worthy literary subjects which emerged from this Romantic racialism. The wave of interest in black subjects among novelists and dramatists has been often mentioned as one of the more remarkable phenomena of the 1920s. The best known example of the use not only of a black subject but one drawn from Haitian history is Eugene O'Neill's play *Emperor Jones* which opened in New York in 1920. O'Neill's play is singular in its attempt to see a black protagonist not simply as a natural primitive but in terms of a larger human tragedy. In some respects it does bring to mind the preoccupation with frenzied jungle rhythms and primal mystery that was fashionable at the time. However, it is ultimately about man's precarious hold on the rational and his inability to impose his will on a universe that is no longer benign.

This use of Haitian material for serious literary purposes is remarkable. Brutus Jones seems to be a composite of Henry Christophe and Guillaume Sam, or perhaps a character torn by the conflict between the grand delusions of the former and the petty, vengeful despotism of the latter. The reference to Haiti is even clearer as O'Neill describes the Caribbean island over which Jones rules as 'yet not self-determined by the white Marines'. This use of Haitian themes to depict a journey into the forest of the unconscious is a unique departure from the cult of the primitive that could only serve to justify the 'salutary lesson' that the Occupation was expected to administer to Haitians.

Even if our main concern is America's reaction against or fascination with the 'looking glass' world of Haiti, we must not lose sight of the fact that in a more general way the lure of primitivism and notion of racially determined cultures were the dominant ideas of the decade. For instance, Lucien Lévy-Bruhl, whose *Primitive Mentality* was available in the United States in 1923, was one of the foremost proponents of the prelogical nature of the primitive mind. Such notions of racially determined cultures were espoused by groups as diverse as Nazi ideologues in Germany, Barrès and Maurras in France, and the négritude writers in the Thirties. These ideas were not discredited until after World War II when a reaction against Nazism facilitated the spread of notions of culture as determined by history and environment rather than race.

RIMBAUD'S 'NÈGRE' AND THE HAITIAN QUEST FOR AUTHENTICITY

> Oui, j'ai les yeux fermés à votre lumière. Je suis une bête, un nègre.
>
> A. Rimbaud, *Mauvais Sang*

As we have seen, the Occupation reinforced many stereotypes that had been fixed in the American imagination from the nineteenth century. Whether seen as a salutary derangement for the fatigued Western psyche or as an illustration of the shiftlessness of the black race, entering Haiti meant a plunge into a dismaying or possibly thrilling looking glass world. Haiti was a place of romance, haunting memories, exotic beings and career advancement. Haitian reactions to American culture and Anglo-Saxon values were also dramatically sharpened during the Occupation.

Prior to the Occupation Haitian attitudes to the United States were characterized by a nervous distrust of American intentions. However, the American never enters as an important figure in Haitian writing until the arrival of the Marines in 1915. This is quite understandable since Americans were not highly visible in Haiti and when Haitians travelled, it was usually to Paris. However, after 1915 the unmistakeably pseudo-colonial nature of the American presence in Haiti sharply defined the image of the American in the Haitian imagination. This does not explicitly emerge in Haitian writing, however, until the 1930s when censorship was less rigidly enforced. Yvette Gindine explains in her survey of the literature of this period:

> Although the Yankee had since 1915 become a ubiquitous military and civilian presence in Haiti's daily life, censorship, imposed or self-administered, prevented his being depicted directly until the last phase of detente (1930–4).[21]

This is largely the case. However, Fernand Hibbert's short novel *Les Simulacres*, published in 1923, is probably the first Haitian attempt to come to terms imaginatively with the American presence. It is not an attack on the Occupation but a bitter satire of political opportunism and deceit within Haiti. Its title could be translated as *The Children of Sham*. By focusing on the machinations of the voluble, megalomaniac politician Hellénus Caton, Hibbert implies that the Americans mercifully put an end to corruption in Haitian politics. Through the level-headed and scholarly figure of Brion, Hibbert advocates that Haitians should make an effort to accommodate their uninvited American guests even if the latter are 'taciturn and sullen' in manner.

Before long, accommodation gave way to resentment. Hibbert's epilogue, written well after the completion of the novel, criticizes the Americans as 'Les Exploiteurs des Faibles'. Also, further insight into the nature of the Haitian reaction can be indirectly gained from the stubborn insistence among Haitian writers on what they saw as their 'latin' sensibility as a means of resisting the American presence. As a reaction against what was stereotyped as the 'arriviste' and materialistic values of the Americans, Haitians adhered to what they saw as the refinements of 'Classical' civilization. The image of an aloof and erudite Haitian culture was opposed to the uncultured, brutish American. This is nowhere more apparent than in the mannered and ornate verse which was cultivated by Haitian poets in the 1920s. The insistence on the use of stately and sonorous alexandrines and high-sounding language was a way of asserting links with Europe and demonstrating Haiti's sophisticated intellectual culture in the face of national humiliation.[22] The high-minded, exhibitionist verse served the nationalist cause in its own way because it managed to soothe the Haitian intellectual's damaged self-esteem. However, as the resistance to the American occupation intensified, the quest for what constituted an authentic Haitian culture acquired greater urgency. At this time the ideas of Charles Maurras in particular had gained great currency and the belief in the shaping power of the genius or 'geist' of the native culture was central to the question of racial stereotyping.

What emerged in such a context was an abstraction called Haiti's afro-latin soul. Cross-fertilized by French and African elements, it was characterized by an emotional intensity, spontaneity and expressiveness which stood in stark contrast to the bland, inhibited world of Western culture. To some extent Haitians were unwittingly miming the stereotype imposed on them by travel writers. For instance, in opposition to America's 'civilisation de feraille, de ciment et de linoleum' Stephen Alexis in his novel *Le nègre masqué* offers 'cette divination nègre des cadences, cette harmonie dépouillée et libre, presque religieuse'[23] (that black instinct for rhythm, that harmony which is unrestrained, free and almost religious). The writing of this period is dominated by these antithetical images of debilitating materialism on one hand and an organic, sensual world on the other. It is also not surprising that many of the plots of the imaginative literature of the time should turn on the difficulties of marrying these two different cultures. The unsuspecting Haitian female courted by an American officer is a sentimental image of the actual circumstances of the Occupation. The invariably melodramatic intrigue, usually set in an urban millieu, is completed by the slighted Haitian suitor who tries desperately to wrest his beloved free from the American's predatory embrace. Examples of the Haitian abhorrence of any such union can be found in a number of novels in the 1930s – such as Leon Laleau's *Le Choc* (1932); Virgile Valcin's *La Blanche*

Négresse (1934), Stephen Alexis' *Le nègre masqué* (1938) and most explicitly in Duraciné Vaval's short play on a dialogue of cultures *Mariage Hatiano-Américain* (1933).

The allegorical presentation of the Occupation in terms of unfulfilled sexual alliances necessarily includes two stock characters: the victimized upper class female and the clumsily amorous officer. The *raison d'être* of this drawing-room fiction is overt anti-American feeling and its purpose is to demonstrate that the American's sexual advances are destined to remain unrequited. The savage caricature of the Marine officer in these works is equalled only by the unmitigated scorn that is directed against those Haitians who collaborated with the Americans. The two most obvious examples of works that present a grotesque image of the American officer are Laleau's *Le Choc* and Alexis' *Le nègre masqué*. Interestingly, both Laleau and Alexis create heroes who ultimately leave Haiti for France, thereby demonstrating the superiority of the latter over the oppressive and mercenary presence of the American.

The nature of this presence in all its racist arrogance is conveyed through the characters of Smedley Seaton and Lieutenant Martin in *Le nègre masqué* and *Le Choc* respectively. Both officers predictably compete with the Haitian male protagonist of the story for the attentions of the latter's beloved. The female of Alexis' story offers an interesting variation since she is French and consequently even more worthy of being gallantly defended. Examples abound of the high-handed and racist attitudes of the American military. A typical example can be found in *Le Choc* where the following remark is uttered:

> Vous haissez les Américains. Nous le savons. Nous ne serions jamais venue ici, si vous n'étiez pas des singes. Nous sommes venus vous civiliser.[24]

> (You hate Americans. We know that. We would never have come here, if you were not monkeys. We have come to civilize you)

Smedley Seaton is an equally unsavoury character whose reactions to Haitians range from unspeakable racism to a self-serving paternalism. Written with an upper-class Haitian audience in mind, these works directly addressed the dilemma of the educated, urban Haitian and offered, vicariously at least, a spiritual victory over the Americans who had triumphed in the short term because of their superior strength.

Nevertheless, there is an alternative rendering of Haitian–American relations in which the American officer is seduced or even overwhelmed by the culture he has come to possess. This theme first appears in Annie Desroy's *Le Joug* which was written in 1931. Possibly the most distinctive feature of this novel is that it is a rare instance of an outsider used as the author's 'porte-parole' in Haitian literature. Colonel Murray, described as 'indigénophile' shares none of the prejudices of his fellow officers and in his sympathetic attitudes to Haitians, he echoes many of the sentiments found in Edward Beach's novel *The Last Haitian Revolution* (cf. pp. 25–7).

What is most remarkable about this character is that he is presented as a spokesman for black nationalism. Murray is, for instance, not against the Occupation but sees it as having a salutary effect on a socially and politically stagnant Haiti. It permits the masses of Haitians to have a say in their society. Desroy, through her character, sees the true villain of the Haitian situation not as the American officer but as the Haitian élite. Murray's arguments for greater cultural and political authenticity in Haiti are akin to those of Price-Mars and the 'Griot' movement. His remarks on the subject of vaudou make his ideological alignment even clearer. He rejects Seabrook's *Magic Island* as an indignity to Haitians. He also argues the case for a revaluation of Haitian culture around its African base.

> Votre idéal est latin et vous êtes nègres . . . il faudrait pour votre évolution affirmer votre personnalité, c'est à dire ne jamais abandonner l'idée que vous êtes tous des nègres sans aucune distinction des nuances.[25]
>
> (Your ideal is latin and you are black . . . for you to evolve, you must assert your personality, that is never abandon the idea that you are all black with no subtle distinctions.)

Desroy's protagonist goes on to make a case for a black head of state.

> . . . Evidemment les 9/10 de votre peuple étant noire, il fallait la representation noire . . . Mais relisez votre histoire. . . . Même

quand la face était noire, la tête et les bras étaient mulâtres. Voilà pourquoi le reste pourrissait dans l'incurie et la misère.[26]

(. . . Since 9/10 of your people are visibly black, you need to be represented by a black man. . . . But reread your history. . . . Even if the face was black, the head and arms were mulatto. That is why all the rest were rotting in negligence and misery.)

Le Joug provides a remarkable insight into Haitian–American relations, since it demonstrates the extent to which the black nationalist cause saw in the Occupation an opportunity for advancing ideas on political and cultural authenticity in Haiti. Haitians no longer wanted to see themselves as New World Quixotes. Their self-image was now assertively black.

In Desroy's narrative an American officer succumbs willingly to the Haitian milieu. In Luc Grimard's short, ironic tale 'Les deux couleuvres de Crackson' another officer is overwhelmed, in spite of himself, by the magic of the Haitian heartland. Grimard tells the story of an American, Lieutenant Crackson, who in his overweening self-confidence epitomizes the smugness and arrogance of the American military. In his expansive exuberance he is by no means as appealing as Desroy's character. In order to win a bet, Crackson sets off into the Haitian interior in order to capture a snake which is considered sacred by the inhabitants of the region. His quest is symbolic of the attempt by cynical invaders to desecrate the soul of Haiti. The lieutenant is, not surprisingly, unsuccessful as his car mysteriously overturns and he is seriously injured, just when he thought he had captured the snake. The would-be iconoclast is taught a lesson and the supernatural has its revenge. In the final scene of the story the peasants gaze in silent triumph at the hapless American pinned under his car.

. . . toutes les horreurs de la corvée de 1918–1920, toutes les tueries, les cabanes incendiées avec leurs occupants, tout en cette minute était là sur la route, entre les spectateurs émus et les victimes muettes.[27]

(. . . all the horrors of the 'corvée' from 1918–1920, all the murders, the cabins burnt along with their occupants, it was all there on the road, between the excited spectators and the silent victims.)

The American, once garrulous now silent, once the master of technology now crushed under the weight of his car, has fallen victim to the subversive wisdom of the Haitian heartland. The final image of the magical snake basking in the Haitian sun, its secret intact, brings to a close this tale of the triumph of peasant values.

In the same way that Rimbaud in 'Mauvais Sang' asserts himself as 'other' – 'Je est un autre' – as 'nègre' in order to defy the values of clarity and order, Haitian resistance to the American Occupation ultimately expressed itself in terms of the figure of the authentic 'nègre'. Alexis 'nègre masqué' had been finally unmasked as the precocious, black 'enfant terrible'. The use of the ingenuous outsider, of the primitive innocent to criticize establishment values is not unusual. This device reappears in the work of Voltaire, Melville and Albert Camus – to cite some of the better-known examples. As C. L. R. James concludes in his study of Melville's *Moby Dick*, the figure of the wise savage was

> . . . a practice which for centuries had been followed by some of the very greatest writers of France and Britain. They were using the primitive savage in his presumed nobility and innocence of vice, as a stick with which to beat the constantly increasing injustices, suffering, deceptions and pretences which seemed to grow side by side with the growth of civilisation.[28]

What is particularly relevant in Rimbaud's use of this persona is his assumed identity as 'poète-nègre'. He offers the values of the sacrilegious barbarian as a way of breaking free from the destructive virtues of European civilization. In the same way that he invoked the 'bad blood', the primal heritage of his Gallic ancestry, the persona of the youthful subversive, the iconoclastic 'nègre' is used during the Occupation in order to counter the objectives of America's 'civilizing mission'.

Younger Haitian writers quickly shed the trappings of the urbane, fastidious 'latin' culture so prized by their forebears and replaced it with the shocking nudity of their African past. The upper-class drawing room or book-lined study has been replaced by the primeval bush. Long-winded eloquence is shattered by a primal scream. Their African ancestry had been textualized in the images of Rimbaud's 'Mauvais Sang' which fiercely extolled the virtues of

... l'idolâtrie et l'amour du sacrilège; – oh! tous les vices, colère, luxure, – magnifique la luxure; – surtout mensonge et paresse.[29]

(idolatry and the love of sacrilege; – oh! all the vices, anger, lust – wonderful lust; – especially lies and sloth)

Salvaging the intoxicating legacy of the ancestral past is a major theme of this new bellicose discourse that had emerged in Haitian writing. The values of the Christian West are ridiculed in images that provocatively promote the virtues of self-indulgent transgression. An iconoclastic hysteria now not only characterizes but authenticates the literary utterance. For instance, Carl Brouard's poem 'Nostalgie' is the best known example of this fascination with the world of the authentic 'nègre'.

> Tambour
> quand tu résonnes
> mon âme hurle vers l'Afrique
> Tantôt
> je rêve d'une brousse immense,
> baignée de lune
> où s'échevèlent de suantes nudités
> Tantôt d'une case immonde
> où je savoure du sang dans des crânes humains.[30]

> (Drum
> When you resound
> my heart howls for Africa
> Sometimes
> I am dreaming of a mighty jungle
> bathed in moonlight
> of naked, sweating, dishevelled bodies
> Sometimes of a filthy hut
> where I savour blood from human skulls)

Calculating in its 'amour du sacrilège', Brouard's poem uses the drum beat sound of 'tantôt' to evoke one grotesque fantasy after another. 'Nostalgie' is a wild plunge into nature, a demonic 'fête champêtre' in which the poet as satanic gourmet perversely mocks the holy Eucharist. The filth, the priapic delirium and the blasphemy of Brouard's defiant poem shows the extent to which the old ideal of the self-absorbed and bookish poise of the francophile Haitian intellectual had been transformed. The masked 'nègre' had metamorphosed into the authentic 'nègre'. Not all the writers of Brouard's generation are as extreme and bizarre as he is. However, the need to strip oneself of the trappings of European culture and to come to terms with the reality of Africa within the self is a consistent feature in writing at the time. Philippe Thoby-Marcelin in 1926 declared 'un éternel dédain aux raffinements européens' (an eternal contempt for European refinement) and expressed the need to

> . . . Me dépouiller de tous oripeaux classiques
> et me dresser nu, très sauvage
> et très descendant d'esclaves,
> Pour entonner d'une voix nouvelle le de profundis
> des civilisations pourrissantes.[31]
>
> (To strip myself of classical finery
> and stand up naked, very much a savage
> and very much a son of slaves
> To sing with a new voice the 'de profundis'
> of rotting civilizations.)

Even if the pagan return is not fully realized by Thoby-Marcelin, Rimbaud's longing for Otherness, the liberating dream of the unencumbered 'enfant terrible', is still the source of the discourse used by militant Haitians to subvert America's 'civilizing mission'. What the poet Léon Laleau was to call 'de coeur obsédant . . . qui m'est venu du Sénégal' (this obsessive heart . . . which has come to me from Senegal)[32] had become by the end of the Occupation the point of departure for the ideology of 'negritude' in Haiti.

'Les blancs débarquent' and Rimbaud's existence as 'nègre' is threatened in 'Mauvais Sang'. In Haiti the Marines disembarked and the authentic 'nègre' was discovered. Haitians now had a sense of being looked at and defended themselves by showing how resistant they were to the 'light' that had been brought to their 'darkness' by the Occupation. Haitian writers produced a discourse in defiance of the aims of the American occupation and celebrated a new symbolic order that in positive terms invoked the curse of Ham, the realm of the defiled body and the disorienting myth of Caliban's primordial Otherness.

3
Dreaming the Same Dream: Harlem, Haiti and Racial Solidarity

FROM HUGHES' DREAM TO HURSTON'S NIGHTMARE

> To fling my arms wide
> In some place of the sun,
> To whirl and to dance
> Till the white day is done
> Then rest at cool evening
> Beneath a tall tree
> While night comes on gently,
>   Dark like me –
> That is my dream!
>
>   Langston Hughes

White America in developing a self-concept based on Reason and Power found it necessary to impose mental boundaries which consigned other cultures to impotence and irrationality. This cognitive map, which became a way of ordering geo-political reality, was shaped by imaginative and ultimately political constraints which marginalized other cultures. Haiti had clearly become by the early twentieth century one of the victims of the shaping force of this discourse. Haiti had been identified as deviant and banished to the cultural periphery. The perception of Haiti in reductive, ideologically determined terms had inexorably led to political attitudes of exclusion, paternalism and occupation.

However, American blacks, themselves victims of this marginalizing discourse, would always find it difficult to perceive Haiti in terms of Otherness. Instinctive solidarity between these communities was virtually assured because they were both racially and culturally defined within a framework of biological determinism and moral disapproval. Consequently, the black American response to Haiti would be, for the most part, more generous in imaginative terms and less of an inflexible monologue based on the subordination of the Other. The polarizing impulse, so much in evidence until now, would yield to the possibilities of genuine dialogue, surprisingly facilitated at times by racial mythification.

The racial and cultural affinity between black Haitians and black Americans had become a constant source of speculation in the early twentieth century. Harlem was in vogue – it was a safe safari into the world of the primitive. The Harlem nightclub like the Haitian voodoo ceremony had become a plunge into the unknown, a salutary disorientation for those who were willing to indulge their wildest fantasies. For instance, Nathan Huggins in his account of the Harlem Renaissance quotes the French travel writer Paul Morand on this subject. Morand, with his keen eye for black authenticity and convinced of the therapeutic value of black culture, praised Harlem because it was living proof of the fact that men could 'live without bank balances, without bath tubs'. He dramatically illustrated his view of Harlem as a miniature Africa by pointing to the erect white policeman as the one obstacle that prevented Harlem from fully reverting to its atavistic past, from becoming a 'Haiti, given over to Voodoo and the rhetorical despotism of a plumed Soulouque'.[1]

Morand's fantasy would not be enough to reassert the latent solidarity that existed between black Americans and Haitians. Links between Harlem and Haiti would be established because of the specific circumstances of the American Occupation of Haiti. At this time, it was black Americans who took the initiative. They were among the first to rush to Haiti's defence when the American Marines landed in 1915. Haitians, at least initially, were unaware of the spontaneous support they would receive from American blacks in their campaign to free Haiti from American domination. Their reaction to black Americans seemed frozen in the smug superciliousness that prevailed in the late nineteenth century. Morand, during a trip to Haiti in December 1927, lamented the fact that the blindly Francophile prejudices of Haitians made them incapable of appealing to black Americans for support.

Les Haïtiens sont si Latins avant d'être Noirs, qu'il ne leur vient même pas à l'idée d'entrer en contact, pour se défendre contre l'emprise américaine, avec les électeurs noirs du parti démocrate américain, ni avec la société pour l'avancement des races de couleur. Personne ici ni lit ou ne connaît même de nom, *The Crisis*, *The Chicago Defender* et les grands journaux de couleur américains. Et pourtant, par qui les Haïtiens seraient-ils mieux compris et défendus que par leurs frères?[2]

(Haitians are so latin before being black, that the thought never occurs to them to make contact, in order to defend themsleves against American domination, with the black supporters of the American Democratic Party, nor with the Association for the Advancement of Coloured People. No one here reads or even knows by name, *The Crisis*, *The Chicago Defender* and the major black American newspapers. And yet, by whom would Haitians be better understood and defended than their brothers?)

Morand was exaggerating a little in his concern over the lack of solidarity between Haitians and their American brothers. In general though Haitians did tend to maintain a high-minded seclusion. However, for black American writers and intellectuals such parochialism was a thing of the past. For instance, the October 1927 edition of *Opportunity* carried the following statement, which pointed to a growing sense of international racial solidarity that had emerged among black Americans.

> The Anglo-African, that is the English speaking Negro, both in America and in the British possessions, is becoming internationally minded with regard to his blood brethren. The World War, the Pan-African Congresses, fostered with prophetic vision by Dr. Burghardt DuBois, the phantasmagoria of the Garvey program, René Maran's *Batouala*, increase in European travel, had forced the international thought both upon the Negro intellectuals and the Negro masses.[3]

The burgeoning sense of Pan-African solidarity was an essential ingredient in the black Renaissance movements of the 1920s. The main figures in these movements were compulsive travellers, who had adopted the spirit of the modern in its taste for the fleeting and the transitory, its insatiable curiosity and its posture of moral and imaginative liberation. Claude McKay fondly depicts this world of the bohemian and the vagrant in the cosmopolitan atmosphere of inter-war Paris. His memoirs *A Long Way From Home* (1937) are not the lament of a 'motherless child' but rather a jubilant celebration of restlessness and self-discovery in a new global community.

> Negroids from the United States, the West Indies, North Africa and West Africa, all herded together in a warm group. . . . It was good to feel the strength and distinction of a group and the assurance of belonging to it.[4]

Paris became the centre for this new sense of racial solidarity and a writer such as René Maran played a pivotal role in ensuring that black writers, students and intellectuals from Africa and the Americas met each other.[5]

Black American admiration for Haiti seemed to focus exclusively on the War of Independence until the American Occupation sparked new interest. Haiti was consistently depicted by black writers as exemplary in its assertion of black nationalism and racial defiance. For instance, in contrast to the number of white journalists who urged intervention in Haiti, we find that black Americans always insisted that Haiti's sovereignty be preserved at all costs. The Haitian president in John Durham's *Diane, Priestess of Haiti* (1902), who is described as 'dreaded but comely and distinguished' declares openly

> We are a nation of blacks. We prefer our independence with all its present shortcomings, to the bonds which white civilisation under the present system of commercial exploitation would bring to us.[6]

Durham's laboriously melodramatic tale also refers to the American taste for sensationalism. An American journalist Mr. Wiley who is predictably clumsy and insensitive, asks for '. . . a good Voodou story, eating babies and all that sort of thing'. Durham's story avoids such cheap sensationalism and is based on historical and political realities such as the army's role in Haiti and the power of German commercial interests. Nor surprisingly, this feeling of racial solidarity would intensify with the American Occupation of 1915. From as early as August 1915, W. E. B. Dubois wrote to President Wilson stating that he was 'deeply disturbed over the situation in Hayti' and wished to be reassured that the government had 'no designs on the political independence of the island and no desire to exploit it ruthlessly for the sake of selfish business interests here'.[7]

Dubois' efforts did not stop at polite requests that American intentions should be benign in Haiti. As editor of *The Crisis* he publicized the events in Haiti and in the editorial of September 1915 he urged that black Americans should be more sensitive to the plight of Haitians '. . . it is not time or place for us American negroes who seldom have had courage to fight, to point scornful fingers at our brothers'. It was also *The Crisis* which sent James Weldon Johnson to investigate reports of injustice emerging from Occupied Haiti. Craige's comment on Johnson's visit to Haiti in *Cannibal Cousins* was predictably scathing and dramatically illustrates the difference in attitudes to Haiti between black and white visitors.

> There was an active American coloured man, a special writer with a grouch (sic) against the white race for social slights, real or fancied . . . jotting down as gospel all the tales told to him by these fanciful, artistic and mendacious people.[8]

However, Johnson's 'jottings' on the Occupation represent a penetrating look at the realities of Occupied Haiti and close examination of the motives that lay behind American involvement in Haiti.

His reports, published in *The Crisis* and *The Nation*, were sympathetic to the Haitian people. He referred to the latter as clean, thrifty and hospitable. His sober accounts of Haitian life from the huts of the peasants to the villas of the élite differ remarkably from the images of outlandish *joie de vivre* prevalent in travel books at the time. His attitude to the Haitian élite was an admiring one. He described them as 'educated, cultured and intellectual' and 'a genuine demonstration of the inherent potentialities of Haitian society'. In contrast, he noted that the American officers where 'rough, uncouth and uneducated, and a great number from the South'. The racial prejudices of the latter were a further illustration of the unjust and neo-colonial nature of the American presence.

Johnson's coverage of the Occupation highlighted two important issues – the unconstitutional nature of the American intervention and the commercial motivation behind it. The directness of his language reveals his outrage at American interference in Haitian affairs. His objection to the Occupation was unconditional.

> For the seizure of an independent nation, we offered the stock justifications: protection of American lives and American interests, and the establishment and maintenance of internal order. Had all these reasons been well founded, they would not have constituted justification for the complete seizure of a sovereign state at peace with us.[9]

To Johnson, the continued American presence was not part of an idealistic enterprise but the result of a crass commercial exploitation of Haiti. As he wrote in *The Nation* in 1920 '. . . To know the reasons for the present political situation in Haiti . . . it is necessary to know that the National City Bank of New York is very much interested in Haiti'. He could not see how authoritarian, military control of Haiti in the interests of the National City Bank could inspire a longing for democracy in Haiti and establish internal stability.

Johnson's conclusion was predictable. The injustice of the Occupation was both constitutional and racial. In 1920 he offered the recommendation that the United States . . .

> Should get out as well and as quickly as it can and restore to the Haitian people their independence and sovereignty. The colored people of the U.S. should be interested in seeing that this is done, for Haiti is the one best chance that the negro has in the world to prove that he is capable of the highest self-government.[10]

Haiti was clearly still regarded as the place where the black man could achieve his highest potential. Haiti's historic mission was perhaps the most important reason behind his objection to the Occupation. In tangible ways Johnson helped to hasten the end of American intervention in Haiti since his reports provided Senator Warren Harding with evidence of the poor handling of the Occupation by the Wilson administration. His activism not only alerted Americans to the painful reality of the Occupation but helped organize Haitian protest against the American presence. He advised Georges Sylvain to organize *L'Union Patriotique* along the lines of the NAACP. Johnson's relationship with Haiti in the 1920s is remarkably similar to that of Frederick Douglass in the late nineteenth century.

After Johnson's visit black American contacts with Haiti, personal, literary and political, intensified. For example, Walter White, who replaced Johnson as Secretary of the NAACP, also visited Haiti like his predecessor. White also reacted with alarm to the injustice of the Occupation in an article 'Danger in Haiti' in the July 1931 issue of *The Crisis*. Similar sentiments can be found in Rayford Logan's 'The New Haiti' in the April 1927 number of *Opportunity*. Logan attacked the propaganda spread at the time by a certain Elwood Mead who presented Haitians as cannibals, 90 per cent of whom were infected with syphilis. The stereotype of Haiti as an infected body turns up with depressing frequency in the twentieth century. Logan was incredulous and became an important voice in attempting to set the record straight. The more general sensitivity to Haiti's situation among black Americans provoked several demonstrations in Harlem. One dramatic example of the solidarity is the reaction to the Haitian student strike at Damiens in 1929 which gave rise to protest marches in the United States and the involvement of the *Save Haiti League*.

It is in the late 1920s that the links between Haitian intellectuals and their black American counterparts would be firmly established. Dubois, Johnson, Logan and Locke are the best known of a number of black American visitors to Haiti at the time. There was a response from some of the more established men of letters at the time, such as Georges Sylvain and Dantes Bellegarde. The latter participated in the Second Pan-African Congress in 1921 and was enthusiastically received by Locke and Dubois.[11] Bellegarde also published in December 1927 an article critical of the Occupation which appeared in *Opportunity*. His article 'Haiti under the rule of the U.S.' echoes most of Johnson's sentiments. They both were convinced that a sophisticated but fragile Haiti had been crushed by a crude and expansionist neighbour. Like Johnson, Bellegarde glossed over Haiti's chronic instability which he dismissed as 'passing trouble' and emphasized the predatory and grasping nature of America's action. Early contacts between black Americans and Haitians in the 1920s took the form of essentially formal and polite exchanges between men who favoured the élite as a solution to Haiti's problem. The second and perhaps more intense phase of this relationship would bring together younger and more iconoclastic Haitians and the radical young men of the Harlem Renaissance. The restless, compulsively vagrant members of the Harlem Renaissance were not interested in Haiti's Francophile élite but in the rural, the archaic and the dispossessed. Langston Hughes' visit to Haiti was startlingly different from that of Johnson. Hughes did not make contact with the élite during his visit to Haiti but concentrated his attentions on the peasants and the urban poor. As a self-styled proletarian 'flanêur', Hughes saw a Haiti that was vastly different to that seen by Johnson. His reports on Haiti in the 1930s infuriated the Haitian bourgeoisie. We get some idea of the impact of Hughes' articles on Haitians when in 1934 *Haiti-Journal* published an angry reponse to Hughes entitled 'Un nègre Américain nous abîme'. The article mentions 'ce mépris du nègre américain pour notre élite . . .'[12] and dismisses Hughes as a misguided communist. The Haitian élite was furious because of Hughes' depiction of Haitian society as the absurd juxtaposition of barefoot, malnourished peasants and a corpulent, well-heeled élite. The tone of Hughes' articles was not bland and respectful as was Johnson's. Hughes offers an insight into social stagnation and colour prejudice dominated by an educated, pampered caste which squandered government money and spent its time writing flowery and high-minded verses. Hughes' bitterly satirical account of Haiti would both mean for relations between Haitians and black Americans a more critical and outspoken phase and an introduction of militantly radical ideas that would influence younger Haitian writers.

Hughes concentrated on two elements in Haitian society – 'The White Shadows' and 'The people without shoes'. In the case of the former, he published a short essay in *The Crisis* in which he examined the white shadows that had fallen across a black land. Naturally, he was referring to the American Marines in Haiti but the white shadows do include the bourgeoisie which had become blindly eurocentric.

> The White Shadows began to fall across the land as the dark aristocracy became cultured and careless, conceited and quite 'high hat'. Today, the Marines are there.[13]

In his own mocking way, Hughes wished to make Haitians aware of their responsibility for the tragedy of the Occupation. They would have none of it. It is not that Hughes was unaware of Haiti's historic significance. He describes with appropriate awe the achievement of Christophe's Citadelle and Haiti's 'thrilling history of the slaves who drove the French into the ocean and freed themselves'. This initial euphoria is restrained because of the way in which Haitians had squandered the promise of the struggle for Independence. In the depressing context of Haiti's new colonial experience, the glory of 1804 seemed remote. Hughes focused his sympathy on the 'people without shoes' who never benefited from independence. The unceasing and cruel exploitation of Haiti's shoeless proletariat moved Hughes intensely.

Haiti was a land of people without shoes – black people, whose feet walked the dusty roads to market in the early morning or trod softly on the bare floors of hotels, serving foreign guests. Barefooted ones tending the rice and cane fields under the hot sun, climbing mountain slopes, picking coffee beans, wading through surf to fishing boats on the blue sea. All the work that kept Haiti alive, paid the interest on American loans, and enriched foreign traders, was done by people without shoes.[14]

Hughes' criticism of the Haitian bourgeoisie and his identification with the working class are consistent with his objection to the black élite in the United States. In Haiti, Hughes deliberately avoided contact with the élite. He moved in a world distant from the fashionable literary salons and experienced the casual arrogance of Haitian officials 'sweating in their tight fitting suits'. He did not use the letters of introduction he had come with. When, on his departure, he is visited by an official delegation of Haitian intellectuals, he noted with amused irritation the contrast between his defiantly bohemian clothes and the formal elegance of his visitors. Given his special approach to the Haitian situation, Hughes' novella *Popo and Fifina* (*Children of Haiti*) published in 1932 is a unique American portrayal of Haiti. Neither respectfully historical nor wildly sensationalist, this plaintive and understated children's book concentrates on the quiet endurance of the Haitian peasantry. A mood of naive wonder and disarming curiosity is prevalent in this story of peasant children starting life in a big town. The text is not overtly political but the children sense that something is amiss in a factory where black workers can pineapples for shipment to the United States.

Here Popo saw many black men working. They did not move about leisurely, like other workers, and Popo thought he wouldn't enjoy working so hurriedly.[15]

Hughes' reaction to Haiti went beyond protest against American intervention. He looked at the society itself and the pernicious combination of class prejudice and economic exploitation that would reassert itself when the Americans eventually left. Hughes' fears were indeed realized when the nationalist spirit created by the American presence was undermined by traditional élite self-interest after the departure of the Americans in 1934.

Relations between black Americans and Haitians in the 1930s were intense and emotional. A picture of President Stenio Vincent appeared in the 31 November issue of *The Crisis*. The end of the Occupation in 1934 caused great elation over the restoration of Haitian sovereignty. However, as Hughes feared, the authoritarian and intolerant nature of Haitian government soon emerged and Stenio Vincent was ironically the one who by the imprisonment of Jacques Roumain in 1934 provoked sharp criticism from black Americans who formerly supported his nationalist ideals. Roumain's imprisonment became a 'cause célèbre' and Hughes was one of the first to appeal to American blacks to rise to Roumain's defence. His letter was published in *The Crisis* of February 1935 under the heading 'Haitian Writer in Jail' and in it he appealed to 'writers and artists of whatever race' to protest immediately against the imprisonment of '. . . one of the very few upper class Haitians who understands and sympathises with the plight of the oppressed peasants of his island home'. A committee was formed to secure the release of Roumain. Three months later *Opportunity* carried an editorial expressing its disapproval of Vincent's despotic regime and its surprise that Haitians who protested against the infringement of their rights by the American government should now deny freedom to their own citizens. The editorial concludes that Roumain's 'trial and conviction smack of dictatorship in its worst aspect. The rights of free speech, free press, free assembly and petition are fundamental rights in a democracy'.[16]

The disturbing political realities of Haiti meant that the dream of racial solidarity would now have to take into account non-racial, historical factors which made instinctive identification between blacks of different societies increasingly difficult. Hughes was perceptive enough to realize that economic and historical factors were potentially more important than race and folklore in assessing a country's experience. This approach was echoed by a few in the 1930s. For instance an article in 1936 published by Harold Preece in *The Crisis* criticized the sentimental approach to black culture and complained about the uncritical acceptance of 'stock premises concerning negro culture'. Preece, a white writer, was perhaps, like Hughes, a little ahead of his time is attempting to destroy the myths of black folk culture. The vogue of folk culture and negro primitivism was still alive and much writing on Haiti was quite different from Hughes' radical Marxism and was meant to celebrate 'the slumbering gift of the folk temperament'.

Haiti features as a theme, a referent for racial and cultural stereotypes that satisfied ideological and exotic needs among many adherents to the New Negro Movement of the 1920s and 1930s. Haiti became overvalued because of its earthiness, its exuberance, its spirituality. It was the most persuasive illustration of a racial *geist*, invoked by many black intellectuals of the New Negro Movement. Perhaps the most famous Haitian protagonist in black American literature is McKay's Ray, portrayed as that whining, repressed Haitian mulatto who is a misfit because he does not have the courage to 'go and lose (himself) in some savage culture in the jungles of Africa'.[17] Ray's heritage is an atavistic longing for the perverse and the carnal which his Westernization never permits him to fulfil. The need to depict Haiti and Haitians as an aboriginal and pre-industrial paradise persisted despite the appeal by a major figure such as Alain Locke to take into account the significance of environmental forces and the process of cultural change in the depiction of black culture. He calls for precisely this in his introduction to *The New Negro, An Interpretation* (1925) in which he declares that the characteristics of American blacks . . .

> are the result of (their) peculiar experience in America and the emotional upheavals of its trials and ordeals . . . they represent essentially the working of environmental forces rather than the outcropping of a race psychology.[18]

In Locke's anthology there is some support for his position from articles like that of Melville Herskovits entitled 'The Negro's Americanism' in which he makes a case for considering Harlem 'a typical American community'. The idea of cultural creolization would not gain currency until the 1940s. In the meantime Locke's remarks would be ignored or simply dismissed, as they were by Claude McKay, as meaningless because of their 'effete European academic quality'.[19]

Haiti was to have a beguiling effect on those who wished to substantiate the peculiar nature of black culture. The special folk values of the New Negro were noted by folklorist Arthur Huff Fauset in Locke's anthology. In seeking to define himself, the black man simply needed to reach back into a folk heritage where '... All nature is alive ... the whispering, tinkling, hissing, booming, muttering, zooming around him are full of mysterious hints and suggestions'. Great effort would consequently be devoted to the recording and documenting of this black folk heritage from the deep South to Haiti. Haiti would become for some the centre of a vortex into which their imaginations would be drawn unresistingly. This view of Haiti as a sensory experience, the source of natural luxuriance, unbridled passion and the power of the supernatural was meant not to establish Haiti's otherness but, on the contrary, its natural, organic relationship to black American folk culture. Haiti would provide for black writers not a shudder of fear but a 'frisson' of recognition.

This celebration of folk values did extend beyond Haiti to include the entire Caribbean. The pages of *The Crisis* and *Opportunity* in the 1920s contain a number of short stories which rather luridly celebrate folk values among Caribbean people. Eric Walrond's tale 'The Voodoo's Revenge' tells of a mysterious poisoning in the Canal Zone. Haitian voodoo – apparently synonymous with any kind of folk magic – is the subject of this macabre story set in a frontier community of Caribbean migrants. Walrond's style is unintentionally comic in its grave and inflated tone used to ennoble the precious world of the folk.

> For hours, as the tropical sun beat down upon them, these lovely angels of Ethiopia would stop and dye their lips with the wine of luscious pomegranates.[20]

The construction of the Panama Canal was a dramatic illustration of the way in which industrial development and the migration of the poor would inexorably affect the folk beliefs of the peasantry. But Walrond is not protesting against the intrusions of modern technology but indulging in a celebration of the supernatural, perhaps provoked – like his contemporary McKay – by a deep nostalgia for the Caribbean he had left behind.

A similar tale of misadventure in a tropical setting is Arthur Fauset's 'Jumby' which was set in Barbados and again focused on the black man's dependence on the supernatural. The power of elemental forces over the individual is everywhere apparent and Fauset's heroine is the incarnation of a kind of muscular sensuality. Her characteristics are more animal than human

> Jean Marie leaped lightly from her bed, and glided to the door of her hut. Her tall slim figure was like a leopard's.[21]

Later, under the spell of the 'jumby', she becomes even more feline.

> Like a panther pierced by the hunter's spear, she leaped from her cot and gliding across the floor of her hut, rushed out into the moonlight.[22]

In these stories the Caribbean is a world of the flesh, of elemental forces, of primordial terror, the epicentre of which was Haiti. They were the English language equivalent of the stories of the Marcelin brothers in Haiti, which were popular at the time. There is none of the 'bold realism' that Locke praised in René Maran's *Batouala* nor the naturalist seaminess of Richard Wright's fiction. There is no story at this time that directly refers to the Occupation. Haiti continued to be textualized either in terms of its legendary, historical past or in terms of a haunting sensuality. This time it was motivated by a misguided generosity based on racial solidarity.

Two works by John Matheus treat Haiti's legendary significance – a short story 'Citadel' (1931) and a one-act play *Ti Yette* (1929). In both works the same basic plot is repeated – that of the tragic mulatto torn between his Westernization and his atavistic impulses. In both cases the male protagonist is confronted with a female character who is callously indifferent to his secret longings. In 'Citadel', published in *The Crisis*, André Solon is inspired by the sight of Christophe's monument and symbolically abandons his French wife to devote himself to recording Haiti's former glory. Matheus wrote elsewhere about the links between Haiti and the English-speaking negro. His play *Ti Yette* is set in New Orleans in 1855 and deals with a male character symbolically named Racine who dreams of returning to his Haitian roots. His assimilationist sister is reluctant to leave Louisiana and her white suitor. The play ends melodramatically with a hysterical Racine stabbing his sister because she has betrayed him. The play closes with the rousing declaration '. . . I am of the race of Dessalines. You shall see that the will of the black man is mightier than the white'.[23]

The most sustained literary representation of legendary Haiti in the 1930s is Arna Bontemps' novel *Drums at Dusk* (1939). This novel recreates the story of the Haitian struggle for Independence. The title sets the tone for the lurid and sensationalist nature of the narrative. The whites are invariably depicted as dissolute and effete while the blacks are grimly sadistic in their thirst for revenge. The novel bristles with violent details and wild acts of revenge, the most startling of which describes a white planter literally blown apart by dynamite.[24] One of the better treatments of the value of Haitian history to American blacks is a little known early story by Ralph Ellison entitled 'Mister Toussan'.[25] It is a witty, irreverent and totally credible tale of some little boys who dream of Toussaint's exploits as a way of dealing with an old white man who does not allow them to pick his cherries. 'Toouzan and not Taar-zan' as the most informed youth declares is not one of the stories in books. Here without the grandiloquence and melodrama of other writers, Ellison quietly establishes the role of Haiti in America's folk tradition and its capacity to provide hope in spite of the oppressiveness of the present.

No account of the impact of Haiti on black Americans in the 1930s can be complete without some reference to Zora Neale Hurston, whose work *Tell My Horse* (1938) is a major effort by a black American to document Haitian folk culture. Like Fauset and other folklorists of this early period, she presented the folk as uncomplicated souls whose lives were dominated by magic and the supernatural. *Tell My Horse* not only deals with folk religion but does touch on political issues. In this regard Hurston has the dubious distinction of being the only black writer who actually approved of the American Occupation. Her biographer Robert Hemenway declares it was her poorest book and openly admits to its shortcomings.

Tell My Horse is filled with political analysis, often of a naive sort, with superficial description of West Indian curiosities. She reports a good deal of public gossip as accepted fact, and she reveals a chauvinism that must have infuriated her Haitian hosts.[26]

Her narrative is reminiscent of the sensationalist travelogues of white American visitors to Haiti. Seabrook is cited approvingly. She consistently praised American intervention in Haiti and dwells on the carnage and anarchy that preceded the landing of the Marines. This meant Haiti's Salvation.

The smoke from the funnels of the U.S.S. Washington was a black plume with a white hope. This was the last hour of the last day of the last year that ambitious and greedy demagogues could substitute bought caco blades for voting power. It was the end of the revolution and the beginning of peace.[27]

Along with this dismaying apology for the Occupation, we find a number of alarming and racist references to the weaknesses of the Haitian character. Hurston's reader is advised that Haitians were compulsive liars 'from the thatched hut to the mansion, the only difference being in the things that are lied about'. She seems to outdo Craige and Wirkus in her description of the unpredictably volatile nature of Haitians who 'are gentle and loveable except for their enormous and unconscious cruelty'. In her definition of the Haitian mentality, she also sees Haitians as untrustworthy. She warns '. . . it is just as well not to pay any money in advance to *anyone* in Haiti unless you know them very well indeed'. There is evidence here of the black American imagination at its least generous.

Her anthropologically questionable study of the Voodoo religion is neither objective nor well organized. Her main aim seems to be to demonstrate the hypocrisy of Haitian society in its refusal to accept Voodoo as a legitimate religion. Her anecdotes were meant to titillate and her reports were influenced by her informants, in whom she seems to have had complete faith. We are treated to stories of Haitian 'mambos' who display their sexual organs in order to permit their followers 'to come face to face with the truth', of the 'black faces' and 'dead eyes' of zombies and confusing references to gods and goddesses. Haiti was for Hurston a nightmare world fit only to be probed anthropologically and to be rehabilitated militarily. Hurston's comments on Haitian folk culture are consistent with her reactionary politics.[28] Other black writers could be forgiven since their sensationalist fictions were often motivated by the urgent need to establish a common folk heritage. Hurston's only motivation seems to have been unmitigated contempt.

In all this, Hughes' image of countless bare feet on hard, dusty roads is one of the more enduring and moving tributes to the Haitian people by a black American. He seems to have been quite alone in his dispassionate and perceptive view of the alienated black masses in Haitian society. For the vast majority, Haiti remained a land of timeless sensuality which either made it more beguiling or provoked a contemptuous sneer. There was a clear need to respond to the specific political reality of Haiti, to measure and classify its culture differently, to remove it from the realm of spectacle. A new urgency and dispassionateness would emerge in the treatment of Haiti in the post-war period. In the meantime, many black Americans still remained imaginatively trapped in a discourse that allowed a fatuous exoticism to mask a far more complex political and social reality. In the 1930s Black America clasped Haiti to its bosom. What was embraced was the 'magic island' of Haiti. What was valorized in the writing of the New Negro movement was Haiti's 'Otherness'. This mythification of Haiti was an important ingredient in Black American self-discovery in the pre-war years. Relations between Harlem and Haiti inevitably trace a visible struggle between the need to know, to understand and the inhibiting constraints of a pervasive imaginative discourse.

HARLEM, FRÈRE NOIR

Quand tu saignes, Harlem s'empourpre mon mouchoir
Quand tu souffres, ta plainte en mon chant se prolonge
Dans le même ferveur et dans le même soir
Frère noir, nous faisons tous deux le même songe

Jean Brierre, *Me revoici Harlem*

Colourful, mysterious, sensual Haiti was central to the discourse devised by black Americans in the 1930s to counter the integrationist and assimilationist tendencies that existed at the time and to assert the organic coherence of the black diaspora. As Michel Fabre points out in his informative study of black Americans in Paris *La Rive Noire*, one of the dominant intellectual figures of the time was Franklin Frazier, whose sociological studies popularized the view that the African element in black American culture had been systematically destroyed during slavery.[29] This view would later yield to that of the anthropologist Melville Herskovits who demonstrated the durability of African survivals in *The Myth of the Negro Past*. In the meantime, Haiti would be used as an antidote to Frazier's hypothesis. The 'cult of hereditism' in the 1930s, as W. B. Williams termed it,[30] made Haiti visible to black Americans. A similarity in concern and outlook would also allow radical Haitian writers to respond to black America's ethnocultural overtures.

Haitians in the 1930s were no longer the Francophile Quixotes of the nineteenth century but unrepentantly 'nègre'. This perception of self enabled the relationship between them and black American militants to intensify and flourish at the time. Radicalized by the experience of the Occupation, younger Haitians violently rejected the establishment values of the Fancophile élite for a new identity based on folk values, cultural authenticity and 'l'âme nègre'. Since Harlem's militants were equally intent on asserting their ancestral heritage, an imaginative discourse allowed Haitians and black Americans to discover each other. The euphoric celebration of an embattled fraternity inspired Jean Brierre to conceive of kindred cultures 'dreaming the same dream'. This passionate feeling for Harlem's writers is apparent from the early 1930s. A character in Maurice Casséus' proletarian novel *Viejo* criticizes his fellow Haitians for ignoring Hughes during the latter's visit to Haiti.

> Cependant, savez-vous seulement que Langston Hugues [sic] a passé trois mois ici, deux mois au cap, un mois à Port-au-Prince, Langston Hugues considéré comme le plus grand poète nègre. Vos clubs ne se sont pas ouverts pour le recevoir, à vos thés il ne fut guère invité . . .[31]

(However, do you know that Langston Hugues spent three months here, two months at Cap, one month in Port-au-Prince, Langston Hugues considered the greatest black poet. Your clubs were not open to receive him, he was hardly invited to your tea parties . . .)

Casséus' passionate defence of Hughes and other black American visitors, who were snubbed by Haiti's Francophile élite, was characteristic of the 1930s but early and important contacts were made much earlier in the late 1920s.

Anti-assimilationism, vital to the New Negro Movement, was also a dominant feature of the literary and political ideology of the 1920s in Haiti. Such a posture facilitated the contact with Harlem's writers. It would be erroneous to see the Haitian preoccupation with indigenous values as a mere miming of the New Negro Movement. This has been an unfortunate tendency among some commentators, such as Janheinz Jahn and Naomi Garret who both saw the Harlem Renaissance as one of the external causes of the indigenous movement in Haiti.[32] Michel Fabre has quite convincingly demonstrated through interviews with the principal figures in the indigenous movement – such as Emile Roumer, Daniel Heurtelou, Philippe Thoby-Marcelin – that little was known of the black American writers before the late 1920s.[33] In any case, Alain Locke in a speech delivered as an exchange professor in Haiti in 1943, does point out that the indigenous movement emerged independently of its black American counterpart. We do have evidence of tentative early contacts between Normil Sylvain for instance and Arthur Spingarn during a trip to the United States in October 1927. This friendship stems from a trip made by Spingarn to Haiti in 1923.[34] Nevertheless, in repudiating their eurocentric past, Haitians in the 1920s had elaborated a cult of naturalness and indigenism, that would be given a more radical, racial twist, when the work of Hughes and McKay became better known. Its earliest manifestation, however, was thoroughly Haitian.

Haitians, humiliated by the American Occupation, needed a new self-image. The mask that provided this new defiant sense of self was that of 'authenticité nègre'. We have seen the early poems of Marcelin and Brouard which celebrate the cult of the hirsute, man-eating ancestor. The aloof and genteel 'homme de lettres' of the past had been replaced by young iconoclasts.

Images of the precocious 'enfant terrible', of the sexual subversive became central to this project of self-definition. Léon Laleau dramatically illustrates this racial stereotyping in these two verses drawn from the 1926 poem 'Atavisme'.[35]

> Si la souple splendeur de votre blanche chair
> Se meurtrit dans l'étau de mes brusques étreintes;
> Si je n'entendis jamais vos agonisantes plaintes
> Lorsque vous vous tordez entre mes bras de fer;
>
> (If the soft splendour of your white flesh
> Is crushed in the vice of my rough embrace;
> If I never hear your cries of anguish
> When you twist between my arms of iron;)

Laleau's carnal and erotic imagery seems ironically expressed in the precious form of a regular rhyme scheme. This verse and the entire poem is structured around a series of antitheses which contrast a limp, frail, feminized white world caught in the brutal embrace of a black male. At the heart of this imaginative network is a reversal of cultural stereotypes. The poem ends with the predictable explanation for the lover's sexual potency.

> C'est que jamais je n'ai senti mes chaudes veines
> Se tempérer de la torpeur des durs hivers
> Et qu'il circule en moi, puissant, âpre et pervers.
> Un peu de ce sang noir des races africaines.
>
> (It is because I have never felt my warm veins
> Cool from the torpor of harsh winters
> And because there flows in me, strong, bitter and perverse
> A little of the black blood of the African races)

Literary radicalism in Haiti meant the emergence of a vengeful carnality. Only other black cultures could respond to Haiti's rough embrace. The yielding texture, the pallid surface of white skin was now inadequate.

Even before seeking this new muscular, male solidarity, Haitians found within Haiti a new Muse. An earthy, sensual, uninhibited 'terre-femme' who could satisfy the new longings. Quite often this female figure was a prostitute, whose experience was a microcosm of the national one. Haiti had prostituted herself to the

Americans and similarly the Haitian 'Muse' had sold her favours to survive. A clear example of this stereotyping can be found in Casséus' *Veijo*. The pervasive theme in his work is that of the price one pays for deserting the land. This is certainly the homily earnestly preached in his book for children *Mambo*. *Viejo* is a more explicit and adult melodrama featuring a Marine called Cap (short for Captain) and a Haitian protagonist who rediscovers himself and his past through 'la première chair connue', his first love who is named Olive. She is the epitome of natural sensuality and despite the fact that she had 'commercialized her favours' during the Occupation, she becomes the route to self-discovery for the rootless protagonist.

The poet who most passionately celebrated this female figure in the 1920s was Carl Brouard. His early verses were shocking revelations of his addiction to what he once called his 'Déesse anthropophage'. This man-eating goddess as she is described in 'Hymne à Erzulie' provokes images of sensual abandon. Her special status is made clear in 'Ma Muse' where she appears in images of violent colour and raucous laughter as a 'Courtisane toucouleure'. Further details are supplied in 'Filles' where the prostitutes introduce themselves in terms of 'regards durs', 'rires canailles', 'caresses brutales'. Love for this female becomes a Baudelairean voyage of damnation. In the poem 'Désir', she overwhelms his sense as he longs to breathe 'l'odeur de femelle' that exudes from her armpits.[36] For Brouard the reversal of ideals is total. Flesh, toughness, stridency become more seductive than the delicate, unspoilt, disincarnate Muse of the past. This representation of the spirit of Haiti in terms of sexual self-assurance is a persistent one in post-Occupation writing. It turns up in a more purposeful and earnest way in the 'hanches robustes' of Annaïse in Roumain's *Gouverneurs de la rosée* and in La Niña in the brothel that is Haiti in Alexis' *L'espace d'un cillement*.

These images are anchored in a specific historical and psychic situation in Haiti. The unstable, vagrant male subject finds a secure place in the restorative, earthy embrace of a woman of the people, the 'terre-femme'. The writers of Haiti's indigenous movement linked in their imaginations sexual adventure and revolutionary action, surrender to the lower (corporeal) stratum with embracing the cause of the lower (social) strata. It is at this point that both the Harlem Renaissance and the Haitian Renaissance, having separately produced an imaginative discourse based on eroticism and populism, meet on common ground. The black poet as erotomane and revolutionary was the order of the day.

The need to assert atavistic impulses made Harlem the American equivalent of a Haitian Voodoo ceremony for Haitian writers in the 1930s. Again Casséus' *Viejo* provides useful illustration of this view. The language used to evoke Harlem's nocturnal pleasures differs in no real way from the wild abandon of the Voodoo dance.

> Harlem, la bruyante joie de faces ternes, bruyante et douloureuse, plaisir sans clarté . . . antichambre de l'Afrique piétinée, mais musique-hall d'une race folle de la joie qu'on lui refuse . . .[37]

> (Harlem, the raucous pleasure of mat faces, noisy and melancholy, joy without light . . . antechamber of downtrodden Africa, but music-hall of a race maddened by forbidden pleasure . . .)

Harlem as privileged site for heightened sensuality in simply another locale where ancestral forces erupt. Voodoo ritual is Haiti's music-hall . . .

> . . . la danse héréditaire ancestrale, la danse que dansait son père nu. . . . La chanson grandit, multipliée, envahit la nuit, roule par toutes les rues . . . cherche la voie qui mène à l'Afrique, patrie de danses noires.[38]

> (. . . the ancestral dance, the dance danced by his naked father . . . the song grows, intensifies, invades the night, rolls though the streets . . . searching for the road to Africa, homeland of black dances)

Harlem and Voodoo, ancestral space that subverts the repressive power of the sleeping city, have a seductive effect on the imaginations of Haitian writers. In forcing these impulses to the surface, a new adventure is embarked upon to establish the emotional reality of racial bonds. The ideal of frenzy, of extreme states of feeling becomes a means of transcending psychological individuality, creative personality and national peculiarities and asserting a broad, new racial consciousness.

The first informed accounts of the Harlem Renaissance by Haitian writers appeared in *La Revue indigène*. In the September 1927 number of this journal, Jacques Roumain, in an interview, laments the fact that Haitians have for too long ignored the 'florissante poésie nègre' of the United States.[39] His example of this movement is the work of Countee Cullen – whose name is spelt 'Countree Cullins'. In the next month's issue of *La Revue indigène*, Dominique Hippolyte translated three poems by Cullen.[40] The interest in Cullen would not last. His verses were too solemn and elevating and technically he tenaciously held on to nineteenth century Romantic forms. His 'Magdaleines noires', for instance, was a tame, idealistic tribute to black prostitutes, dignified by the Biblical reference. It was vastly different from Brouard's celebration of carnal pleasure. Even his most direct and racial poem 'Incident' is more plaintive than aggressive in dealing with white prejudice.

La Relève was to be the magazine that would make the work of the Harlem Renaissance available to Haitians in the 1930s. The choice of representative American poets at this time would be more successful. The unpretentious and defiant style of Langston Hughes, the fierce militancy of a Claude McKay would be more suitable to Haitian tastes than the high-minded pieties of Cullen. From its first number in July 1932 *La Relève* focused on the Harlem Renaissance writers. Jean Price-Mars began a series of articles entitled 'A propos de la "Renaissance Nègre" aux Etats-Unis'. Price-Mars' use of the term 'Renaissance Nègre' is perhaps revealing for 'nègre' implies the fiercely uncompromising nature of what *La Relève* sought in the Harlem Renaissance. Price-Mars' early definition of 'valeurs nègres' sums up the qualities that would be associated with black authenticity – 'intuition pénétrante', 'fraîcheur d'inspiration' and 'réalisme sensuel'. Consequently, the selection of poems made by Haitians centred on 'Valeurs nègres'. The poets found most suitable for this purpose were Langston Hughes and Claude McKay.

The role of René Piquion in determining the image of black American writing in Haiti was significant. It was Piquion who translated the poems of Hughes and McKay. Given Piquion's ideological predilections at the time, the poems chosen would renounce aestheticism for the freshness and spontaneity of the 'génie poétique nègre'. The one exception to this would be Claude McKay's 'Souvenir des Tropiques à New York'.[41] The English original 'The Tropics in New York' first appeared in 1920 and is remarkable because it does not use a linear militant rhetoric so characteristic of his other poems. Nevertheless, it retains a regular rhyme scheme and uses a rather precious poetic vocabulary.

In French the poem is less old-fashioned and the nostalgia poignant. McKay's 'longing . . . for old, familiar ways' is more sentimental than 'affamé de ces choses du pays natal', which is closer to the hedonism of some of Carl Brouard and Léon Laleau's celebrations of racial atavism. McKay's poet weeps but Piquion's misfit 'éclate en sanglots'. However, the theme of the black misfit trapped in a materialistic and repressive white world had become one of the stock themes of the indigenous movement. McKay's poem was stylistically conservative but thematically its success was guaranteed.

It was the poetry of Langston Hughes, however, that appealed to Piquion because it was suitable from both the technical and thematic point of view. Later we would see that Jacques Roumain was drawn to a different side of Hughes and approached American society on quite different ideological terms. The first hint of the power of Hughes' poetry for Haitians in the 1930s can be seen in the third article by Jean Price-Mars on the 'Renaissance nègre'. In this essay Price-Mars chooses 'Our Land' by Hughes for special comment and translates the entire poem. 'Notre Pays', as Price-Mars called it, can be seen as the improved version of McKay's 'Souvenir des Tropiques à New York'. Both poems evoke 'la nostalgie de la vie tropicale' and consequently are remarkably similar to Haitian poems of this period. Unlike McKay, however, Hughes avoids a stately and ornate poetic rhetoric. His poem more palpably captures the mood of alienation because of its spontaneous, spoken quality. The use of repetition is the principal device for conveying the sense of profound estrangement . . . 'Nous devrions avoir un pays d'arbres, / De grands arbres épais' and so on. In poetically appropriating the energies of the spoken voice, Hughes had created an immediate, felt and expressive quality that the Haitian poets of the 1930s saw as an aesthetic ideal.

Réne Piquion took his cue from Price-Mars. Hughes' poetry is exemplary for Piquion because it eschews the erudite and high-minded literariness of the past. His is almost a Rousseauesque repudiation of the written word as a symptom of a corrupt society. The modern black writer should not, according to Piquion, cling to the

... mièvreries, aux fadeurs des temps périmés, à l'académisme désuet, aux procédés anachroniques des écrivains bourgeois, à l'esthétisme et au culte de la forme des décadents.[42]

(preciousness, to the insipidness of former times, to obsolete erudition, to anachronistic techniques of bourgeois writers, to the aestheticism and the cult of form of decadent writers)

Hughes was approved of both poetically and politically. His work epitomized a new international black style which was both emotionally and ideologically engagé, 'une capacité émotionnelle extraordinaire' combined with a 'conception concrète des choses'.

The poems by Hughes that were selected by Piquion and published in *La Relève* invariably glorified the black race. These poems either catalogued the historic suffering of the black race or celebrated the natural beauty of blackness. Hughes became gradually incorporated in the ideological quarrel that had begun to divide Haitians in the 1930s. His poetry was used to reinforce feelings of racial paranoia and to promote the case for a politics based on racial authenticity. For instance, the poem 'Negro' is published twice in the pages of *La Relève* and simply entitled 'Poème' in both 1933 and 1936. Piquion's version of the text is more emphatically black than Hughes' original. Hughes' first verse is

> I am a Negro:
> Black as the night is black
> Black like the depths of my Africa.

The Piquion translation sharpens the tone of longing and the sense of a shadowy existence.

> Je suis Nègre
> Je suis sombre comme la Nuit
> Comme les profondes ténèbres de
> L'Afrique, ma Patrie[43]

The changes in language, tone and graphic presentation are significant. Hughes had been appropriated by an ideological discourse that was peculiar to certain Haitian ideologies in the 1930s.

The alterations made by Piquion to the poems celebrating black beauty are no less innocent. The poem 'My People' was translated by Piquion in 1933 and similar attempts were made to heighten the racial message. Hughes' poem is plaintive in its appeal:

> The night is beautiful
> So the faces of my people.

Piquion's rendering is more pointed and strident:

> Les nuits sont belles
> Comme les visages des hommes de ma Race.[44]

The interest in Hughes rarely transcended the themes of racial nostalgia and revenge. Hughes' Marxist and more universal interests had no appeal for those whose narrow ideological objective was to cleanse Haiti of its inauthenticity. Hughes, the footloose bohemian, champion of an international proletariat, is alluded to in Piquion's biography of Hughes entitled *Un Chant Nouveau* (1940). However, the reading of Hughes' poems made available in the pages of *La Relève* singlemindedly focus on the issue of race. It is difficult not to link Piquion's text of 'Notre Pays' which appeared in March 1934 with his declaration in *La Relève* of April 1934 that dictatorship was . . . 'la raison et la volonté alliées à la Force au service de la nation' (reason and will linked with Force in the service of the nation). Repossession of one's land for Piquion was a more ominous goal than was ever intended by Hughes.

It was not Hughes, the Harlem ideologue, that appealed to that other Haitian writer whose relationship with Hughes was at least as intense. Jacques Roumain saw in Hughes a commitment to the universal struggle of the proletariat. Writing in 1967, Roger Gaillard speculates that Roumain's knowledge of Hughes went back to 1927 and more importantly that Hughes' work and life were among the factors that . . . 'radicalised Roumain's political thought, leading him in 1932 towards Marxism'.[45] The revolutionary idealism of Hughes, compulsive traveller and international activist, finds a clear parallel in the life and work of Roumain. His poem to Hughes is a touching tribute to the latter's ceaseless wandering and humanitarian ideals.

> Tu as promené ton coeur nomade, comme un Baedecker, de
> Harlem à Dakar.
> La mer a prêté à tes chants un rythme doux et rauque, et ses
> fleurs d'amertume écloses de l'écume.[46]

> (Your nomadic heart has roamed, like a Baedecker, from Harlem
> to Dakar.
> The sea gave to your songs a wild sweet rhythm, and its bitter
> flowers born from the foam.)

Consequently, Roumain's treatment of the United States does not focus on Harlem nor on the sensuality and earthiness of black Americans. During his stay in New York (1939–40) he showed greater interest in the current world crisis than in[47] racial solidarity. His essay 'Les Griefs de l'hommes noir' published in 1939 examines the phenomenon of lynching as the product of a system that divides and exploits the poor of America, both white and black. His main idea is that 'un égoisme de classe rapace et sans scrupule' (a rapacious and unscrupulous selfishness based on class interest) is at the heart of racial conflict in the United States. His essay is a piece of orthodox Marxist analysis in thrust and expression which exposes racism as a sentimental offshoot of the class struggle. Racial division was simply the means whereby the economic 'status quo' could be maintained.

> Le préjugé de couleur est un instrument de division des masses laborieuses du sud, blanches et noires, dont les revendications, si elles étaient communes ébranleraient l'ordre établi.[48]

> (Colour prejudice is an instrument that divides the working class of the South, white as well as black, whose demands, if they were unanimous, would shake the established order.)

Consistently in Roumain, the racial question is subservient to that of economic circumstance. This belief shared by Hughes was the basis of their friendship. Roumain's later poems in the collection *Bois d'Ebène* show the evidence of the aesthetic and thematic influence of Hughes in their aggressive spokenness and fierce celebration of the new proletarian dawn. Through Roumain, Hughes would capture the imagination of a public quite different from Piquion's – the imagination of the leftist radicals of 1946, who also saw Haiti in a global context.

By 1940 the bonds between Haitian writers and their black American counterparts had been firmly established. Travel was more frequent and personal ties had grown stronger. For instance, Jean Brierre who studied at Columbia University in the early 1940s and also knew Hughes personally, wrote a number of mood poems, genteel and moving, about the bitter fraternity that bound Harlem and Haiti. In his work, the stock theme of the cold brittle nature of white culture is treated in the context of New York. The noise of New York is evidence of a deep fissure in that world.

> Un soir
> Obsédeé par la remeur hallucinante
> De New York
> Tu m'as dit
> Avec une étrange inquiétude dans le regard
> et dans la voix
> ECOUTE CRAQUER LA CIVILISATION.[49]
>
> (One evening
> Delirious from the clamour
> Of New York
> You said to me
> With a strange disquiet in your look,
> and in your voice
> HEAR THE CRACKING OF CIVILIZATION)

To the poet, locked in his room, the noise of New York streets creates a physical malaise and seems to echo the explosive destruction of World War II taking place at the time.

It is the Baudelairean 'Spleen' poem that Brierre uses to communicate the intimate sense of his secret bonds with Harlem. Neither internationalist in scale nor pointedly ideological, Brierre's poetry focuses on Harlem as a place of anguish and melancholy. In 'Harlem' he lists black America's experiences as 'la peine/le travail/la fatigue/la misère . . . sur la route hostile et noire'. The common denominator of racial suffering was for Brierre the single factor that obliterated the difference between Harlem and Haiti. Feeling stronger than language establishes a sense of shared values.

> Nous avons désappris le dialecte africain,
> Tu chantes en anglais mon rêve et ma souffrance

Au rythme de tes 'blues' dansent mes vieux chagrins,
Et je dis ton angoisse en la langue de France.⁵⁰

(We have lost our African language
You sing in English my dreams and anguish,
To the rhythm of your 'blues' dance my old sorrows,
And I express your suffering in the French language.)

Later poems like 'Black Soul' (1946) and official tributes to Paul Robeson and Marian Anderson in the 1950s would more stridently trumpet the message of racial solidarity. These poems in the grand manner would be fed by the lived experiences of 1942–43 in New York City. The poems of this period are unusual because it is not the glamour and sensuality of Harlem that are celebrated. It is rather the sense of human suffering which allows Brierre to check the didactic impulse and create both a credibility and intimacy in this evocation of Harlem.

Because of the American Occupation Haitians had come face to face with the parochial nature of their past and had opened themselves to other cultures. The United States Occupation, like the Connecticut Yankee at King Arthur's Court, had insisted on forcing material progress on what Americans saw as a backward and superstitious land. In so doing they ensured a hostility among Haitians that created in the latter a sense of common suffering with black communities in the United States and elsewhere. An aloof and supercilious Francophile culture in Haiti had yielded to a more generous attitude to other black cultures. The literary imagination in Haiti showed it was capable of liberating systems of belief and human practice which in the past had imprisoned and isolated Haitians in a false sense of superiority. Haitian reactions to the Harlem writers also demonstrate the complexities of cultural contact. The reading or mis-reading of Hughes' poetry in *La Relève* offers valuable insight into the process of cultural reception. Prevailing ideological constraints in Haiti in the 1930s made for a tendentious translation of Hughes' works and a reduction of American culture to a frenzied Harlem. A stereotyped discourse might both deform the image of a culture as well as make cross-cultural contact possible.

4
Passionate Apologists: Haiti and the United States in the Post-Occupation Years

FROM PERIPHERY TO CENTRE

What came surreptitiously into being between the age of the theatre and that of the catalogue was ... a new way of connecting things to the eye and to discourse.

Michel Foucault, *The Order of Things*

Even after the end of the American Occupation in 1934 Haiti continued to be visible in terms of antithetical extremes – land of promise or land of savagery, where the natives were nobly or ignobly black. Either uncritically idealized or blindly denigrated, Haiti had become the stock in trade for cheap sensationalist fiction, such as Theodore Roscoe's *Murder on the Way* (1935) – a murder mystery complete with voodoo drums and malevolent zombies. However, at the end of the decade, Haitian–American relations entered a new phase. Politically and culturally a new 'order of things' was established, as Americans, like Plato's Cave dwellers, bravely turned away from what appeared to be Haiti's disturbing strangeness and tried to face the reality of Haiti.

Haiti, seen in this new light, was no longer a spectacle. A new kind of curiosity emerged that was no more based on sensory experience but on dispassionate inventory. Haiti's obscurity was probed, measured and catalogued in a meticulous and scientific manner in the late 1930s and early 1940s. For a while sensationalist journalism was supplanted by the scientific monograph and scholarly disinterest triumphed over more than a century of cultural myopia. The ethnographic studies of this period were a conscious attempt to bridge the gap between Self and Other. Ethnography may start with the disturbing appearance of radical differences between cultures but it makes an effort precisely to bridge that gap, to understand the differences. It is likely to eliminate the distinction between Self and Other, observer and observed by showing that apparent differences are trivial and superficial. By shifting point of view and approach, scientific studies of Haiti after the Occupation celebrated the similarity of social and psychological processes that existed in both Haiti and the United States. For a while they made the strange more familiar and, by implication, challenged the image Americans had of themselves. Beneath the surface, it was felt, Haitian and American society manifested patterns of acculturation and evolution that were surprisingly alike. Haiti, no longer marginalized, moved from the periphery to the centre.

This view of Haiti as an exemplary rather than a deviant society was facilitated by, among other things, a major change in American policy in the Caribbean. By the late 1930s the period of 'gunboat diplomacy', actively pursued in previous decades, had come to an end. The policy of aggressive military intervention in Caribbean states, that had made the occupation of Haiti possible in 1915, yielded to a new attitude that questioned the use of military force to bring stability to the Caribbean region. This led to the development of the 'Good Neighbour' policy in the presidency of Franklin Roosevelt in 1933. The withdrawal of American troops from the Dominican Republic in 1924 and Haiti in 1934 was the culmination of this new non-interventionist policy. The need to reinforce good relations between Haiti and the United States was felt by Roosevelt, who set up a project in 1943 to train English teachers in Haiti under the direction of Mercer Cook. Indeed, official relations became so cordial that President Lescot in his inaugural address in 1941 could declare that Haitian policies would 'sincerely and faithfully reflect' those of Haiti's 'generous and powerful neighbour'.

The 1940s also meant a change in attitudes to race in the United States. The 'romantic racialism' of the 1920s had become discredited among black artists and intellectuals, who were now more interested in showing how material conditions determined behaviour and attitudes among American blacks. Langston Hughes' presentation of American blacks as proletarians within an oppressive and unjust global system is an example of the departure from an earlier preoccupation with race. Similarly, Richard Wright's *Native Son* (1940) eschews the unrestrained *joie de vivre* of the early Harlem writers to depict a grim picture of proletarian rebellion against America's 'commodity profit machine'. This tendency to see the racial issue in universal terms was further supported by scholars who, quite often in reaction against Nazi nationalism and racism, felt that environment was the most important factor that determined differences between races.

The rise of this movement towards 'liberal environmentalism' or 'environmentalistic sociology' was noted in Gunnar Myrdal's massive study of the question of race in the United States, *An American Dilemma* (1944). In examining the paradoxical disparity in the United States between high-minded, Christian precepts and the petty and prejudiced nature of private attitudes to race, Myrdal felt that the belief in white superiority was simply a vulgar application of cultural Darwinism. He welcomed the fact that . . .

> the heavily prejudiced position of science on the race problem was beginning to be undermined. Professor Franz Boas and a whole school of Anthropologists had already come out against the argument for racial differences based on the primitive people's lack of culture.[1]

Indeed, Franz Boas was a major figure in pioneering a scientific study of the black race in the United States. For a number of years he had contested the hypothesis of black inferiority. As professor of Anthropology at Columbia University he had encouraged many scholars, including Zora Neale Hurston, to collect information on black folk culture. In his work *The Mind of Primitive Man* (1938) he challenged the speculations of Lévy-Bruhl on the subject of primitive mentality and lamented the lack of serious scientific investigation on the subject of race

> I think we have reasons to be ashamed to confess that the scientific study of these questions has never received support. . . . The investigations of Herskovits on the American Negro are a valuable beginning.[2]

Herskovits' early work on race pleased those who supported a liberal, scientific approach to this question. Even Alain Locke, who had deep reservations about the 'overemphasis on the hypothesis of African culture survivals', welcomed Herskovits' scientific objectivity in *The Myth of the Negro Past* because

> In line with the progressive wing of anthropological scholarship, it attempts considerable and vindicating revision of traditional conceptions of the Negro.[3]

Such an atmosphere of accommodation and understanding on the subject of racial differences would allow Haiti to be seen differently. A new scientific discourse would diminish Haiti's 'Otherness' in the 1940s.

In order to reduce the apparently unbridgeable differences between Haiti and the United States, that either shocked or titillated earlier visitors, post-Occupation writing stressed not only the need to make an effort to see things from the native point of view but also to admit that the 'primitive' lurked in all men of whatever race. Mabel Steedman's attempt to understand Haitian folk religion in *Unknown to the World, Haiti* (1939) laments the sensationalism that was associated with Haiti because . . . 'We live in an age where the public demands sensation'. Her work was an attempt to make the real Haiti 'known to the world'. Unlike many of her prim predecessors Steedman admits to the effect of the voodoo drums which made her realize that 'the primitive lies dormant in all of us'. Her book contains a strong plea for cultural relativity, which would in general prevail in accounts of Haitian culture and society until the advent of Duvalierism in 1957. Steedman still unguardedly refers to Haiti as primitive but argues that serious study must go beyond superficial differences.

> One must not look at primitive religions from a biased point of view; it is imperative to look for the underlying idea and try to see things from the point of view of the people concerned.[4]

In the 1940s Haiti was rediscovered. No longer hostile and bizarre space, it was seen as vital and creative. Several visitors to Haiti at this time stressed the imaginative and artistic energies of the Haitian people. The major phenomenon of this decade was the discovery of Haitian 'primitive art'. In 1943 Dewitt Peters, himself a painter, was included in a group of English teachers who were sent to Haiti by the United States government. On his own initiative and with the financial assistance of the Haitian government, he opened a gallery in Port-au-Prince in 1944. 'Le Centre d'Art' attracted a number of self-taught Haitian painters. Living in hovels, using cardboard canvases and painting with housepaint and chicken feathers at times, they produced works which were startling imaginative fantasies. Peters' gallery was an enormous success and it was not wild voodoo rituals that now attracted visitors to Haiti but the creative power of its people. Another famous visitor, in early 1946, was André Breton who gave his stamp of approval to the wonderful and inventive work of Haitian 'primitives'. Murals painted by the latter and commissioned by the Archbishop in 1949 were used to decorate the Cathedral of Ste. Trinité. Travel books of the period would inevitably refer to this 'discovery of Haitian primitive art' just as in the past the voodoo ceremony would be sinisterly unavoidable. The guidebook and personal chronicle written by Hugh B. Cave, *Haiti, Highroad to Adventure* (1952) is typical of the benign, admiring attitude of those who in the 1940s stressed the creative potential of the Haitian imagination. Haitian art forms were in fashion. Haitian drummers captured international attention and Katherine Dunham introduced the ritualistic and ceremonial elements in Haitian dance forms to the New York stage.

It was not only folk art that attracted attention but literature as well. It was in 1943 that the novel *Canapé Vert*, written by Pierre and Philippe Thoby-Marcelin, won the prize for best novel from Latin America in a contest sponsored by the Pan-American Union. The Haitian writer, like the 'primitive artist', would now be included in the effort to steer clear of old stereotypes and to emphasize the positive aspects of Haitian culture. Not only would the Marcelins be referred to by visitors to Haiti but Jacques Roumain and Anthony Lespès as well. This can be seen in the travel book of Ruth Wilson *Here is Haiti* (1957) in which she declares that Haiti contains 'no poisonous snakes nor plants and no poisonous people as far as their treatment of the stranger within their gates is concerned'.[5] In this regard, the most famous promoter of Haitian literature in general and the Marcelin brothers in particular was Edmund Wilson who visited Haiti in 1949.

Wilson's visit to Haiti is recorded in his travel book *Red, Black, Blond and Olive* (1956). Wilson is not a typically earnest and admiring visitor. He does avoid the sensationalism of earlier writers. For instance, he chooses to visit the UNESCO project at Marbial rather than experience the thrill of primitive nocturnal rituals. Haiti was no 'magic island' to Wilson and he subjected it to a sharp and sometimes patronizing scrutiny. For instance, he admits to the 'interested motives' and 'highhanded procedure' of the American Occupation but justifies it in terms of the material progress it had left behind. He praises the gentleness and charm of the Haitian landscape and the achievements of the Haitian people. He associated closely with the well-heeled Haitian élite and is essentially referring to them when he recommends Haiti for those depressed or discouraged by Harlem or the conditions of the South. 'They will be surprised to discover how stimulating Haiti is . . .' since Haitians 'have made something of their breed'.[6] Not surprisingly, it is not folk culture that attracts Wilson but the elegant and fashionable world of the élite. He insists on the Mediterranean quality of urban life in Haiti and claims that

> the tradition of French manners has made (Haitians) restrained and quiet. In all matters of social relations, the taste of Haitians is perfect. The Haitians rarely raise their voices, and they are usually soberly dressed and decorously behaved.[7]

The distaste he feels for the rest of the population is thinly veiled. There is a high-minded sneer in his description of the illiterate peasantry 'in their primitive mud huts, thatched with banana leaves' living in 'an African jungle, dominated by voodoo divinities'.

Naturally, he shows little interest in folk culture. He does not care for what he terms the 'Voodoo-worshipping peasant'. As far as Wilson is concerned the latter's cultural level needs to be improved. He quotes at length from the 'white converts' to Haitian voodoo. Two works in particular written by Americans who 'fell under the spell of voodoo' are cited. They are Maya Deren's *Divine Horsemen: The Living Gods of Haiti* and *Strange Altars* by Marcus Bach. It is the literate, formal expression of Haitian culture that interests Wilson. He saves his unqualified approval for the novel *Canapé Vert* by the Marcelin brothers. He is scathing about popular culture as he is about populist ideology. Consequently, the work of the Marxist writer Jacques Roumain is dismissed. *Bois d'Ebène* is 'unimportant as literature' and *Gouverneurs de la rosée* is 'a Marxist fantasy'. In contrast, he reserves high praise for the 'important anthropological novel' of the Marcelins. It is the capacity of the Marcelins to go beyond the 'external meagerness of peasant life' and reveal 'the richness of the life of myth' that attracts Wilson. He is not interested in the idealistic reforms of Roumain but in the anthropological perspective of the Marcelins. Wilson himself repeats the image of the inner reality of Haiti which only the anthropological eye could discern. Port-au-Prince is 'at first drab and meager' but on closer scrutiny 'rich in interest'. He approves of the Marcelins because they allow him to glimpse – at a safe distance – the marvellous underside of Haitian reality.

Faith in the value of the anthropological perspective has a special lure in the post-Occupation years. Wilson was no anthropologist, however. He was the epitome of the travel writer. The anthropological approach is an exercise in self-effacement. Wilson's imperial geniality looms large in his observations. The anthropological observer is expected to vanish in the face of his material. Fieldwork must replace the imagination; the commonplace must replace the extraordinary; the objective catalogue must replace irresponsible subjectivity. The vanishing subject is the hallmark of the anthropological work of this time and not the idiosyncratic travel book which gives absolute priority to the observer, as Wilson's does. For Wilson, Haiti was still a curiosity on the fringes of the civilized world. A high-minded patrician attitude is pervasive in his thinly veiled distaste for Haiti's black majority and his admiration for the Francophile poise of the urban élite. The anthropological studies of the post-Occupation period would concentrate on the black majority and tend to ignore the urban sectors of Haitian society. The important American researchers who provided the scientific documentation of Haitian society and culture in the late 1930s and early 1940s were Melville Herskovits, Harold Courlander, James Leyburn.

It is not the bizarre juxtaposition nor the strange profusion of things that prevail in the scientific study of Haiti but a discourse based on similarities between cultures and societies. It is 'Sameness' and not 'Otherness' that determines the new discourse. In this regard, the earliest and most striking work is Herskovits' *Life in a Haitian Valley* (1937). In his anthropological study of the Mirebalais valley, Herskovits is not interested in extolling the benefits of the American Occupation. He chooses for his fieldwork a site 'where the intervention of the United States seems to have passed without any discernible effect' except the crude lettering on the bark of the tree 'L. MARLOW U.S.M.C. DRUNK AS HELL'. This is contrasted to the ornate and dignified inscription on the tombstone of the 'Duc de Mirebalais' who had fought in the war for Haitian independence. The valley is an enduring heartland, a repository for traditional values and historical encounters. The true face of Haiti was for Herskovits vastly different from that which was revealed by Wilson.

Herskovits' objective was a professional one – to chronicle uncharted areas of the Haitian experience. He consequently attacks those who refuse to 'seek well beneath the surface' in order to understand the country and its people. He attacks the lack of tolerance and objectivity that has been shown in the superficial treatment of folk religion.

> ... the untrained observer tends to assess what he sees in almost any terms but those of the underlying discipline that defines all activity in the worship of the gods ... it must be emphasized, despite so much that has been written to the contrary, that this form of worship of the *loa* is neither unrestrained hysteria nor drunken orgiastic satisfaction of the sex drive.[8]

Herskovits' hypothesis is that Haitian voodoo is not 'a grim system of ... frenzied rites and cannibalism' and that Haitians do not live 'in a universe of psychological terror'. Indeed the emphasis in not on Voodoo but on documenting Haitian culture in its varied manifestations – private and public, religious and secular, African and European. Ultimately, Haiti is used to illustrate Herskovits' thesis that the black man did have a past which determined his identity. This interest in cultural retentions is evident from his earliest work, and became the shaping concept in his later work *The Myth of the Negro Past* (1958). This monograph would be an invaluable contribution to the campaign pioneered by Gunnar Myrdal's *An American Dilemma*, which sought to document the black American presence in the United States.

For Herskovits Haiti was not deviant but a model of New World acculturation. It was a dynamic society that had combined both African and European influences to create something new. In the same way that he had stressed the Americanism of the black man in the United States, he now emphasized the Haitianization of the black man in Haiti. He concludes that 'the Haitian negro has by no means been overwhelmed by European tradition, just as he has not retained his aboriginal heritage without any change . . .'. These cultural influences had undergone significant change and it was precisely this process, so discernible in Haitian culture, that would provide a clue to cultural evolution in the United States itself. Haiti was for Herskovits a moment of self-discovery, a way of refuting the fallacies that had dominated the question of race in the United States.

Consequently a knowledge of the strains which came to Haiti, of the manner in which they met the situation they found there and of how the cultural influences that played upon them have worked out in terms of patterns of behavior, should throw light on the way in which American Negroes have met and are meeting their social situation.[9]

Life in a Haitian Valley is ultimately about life in a New World situation. Herskovits neither advocates black nationalism nor blind assimilation but sees Mirebalais as a paradigm for creolization in the Americas.

Another scientific monograph that concentrated on the creativity of the Haitian people was Harold Courlander's *Haiti Singing* (1939). The songs and music were collected in field trips undertaken between 1936 and 1939. Like Herskovits, Courlander steered his reader away from the view of Haiti as bizarre and outlandish. He defined Voodoo, for instance, as the Haitian world view, which shaped the 'relationship of the Haitian to the world of reality, to the world of the unseen as well as the seen'. Courlander's main interest was the music of the Haitian people, which allowed them to coordinate group activity and to preserve traditional customs and practices. Whereas the ancestral past was greatly diminished in other forms of cultural expression, music and dance allowed cultural retention to persist. Because this aspect of culture was not taken seriously by outsiders, its creative and subversive power was never fully understood.

What seems to have attracted Courlander was the relationship between labour and culture, music and working. From the outset, he states 'In Haiti everyone sings and dances. . . . In Haiti everyone works'.[10] Not surprisingly, the newer version of this early work was entitled *The Drum and the Hoe* (1960) – the traditional instruments of music and work. This was an observation that would be shared by the novelist Jacques Roumain who made the relationship between rhythm and collective labour the main idea in *Gouverneurs de la rosée*. Courlander similarly demonstrated that organic rhythms and movement coordinated effort and established a bond between individual and group. Again Haiti was seen as an exemplary, aboriginal community which allowed us insight into the coordinating value of song and its relationship to power over nature and reality. In Haitian music could be seen as the synchronizing capacity of the rhythmic chant and its ability to increase the collective strength of the community.

What Herskovits and Courlander did for Haitian culture, James Leyburn did for Haitian society. Leyburn paid little attention to Voodoo and concentrated on the sharp contrasts that existed between élite and peasantry in *The Haitian People* (1945). His main thesis was that Haitian society was divided into castes.

> The two castes are the elite and the masses.
> They are as different as day from night, as nobleman from peasant; and they are as separate as oil and water.[11]

For Leyburn this was the disturbing truth that lay behind the picturesqueness of Haiti. His heart belongs not with the élite, who are deeply insecure, but the vast majority of Haitians who form the underprivileged caste. He becomes effusive and lyrical where they are concerned 'To know the average Haitian is to feel a warm affection for him. His life is never easy, yet he bears it all with a true beauty of spirit'.[12] In his desire to illustrate the stark and divided reality that lay under the surface of Haitian society, Leyburn made little mention of Haiti's black middle-class. This group had benefited from the opportunities for technical training that had been offered during the American Occupation or had traditional status in Haiti's provinces. Leyburn's image of Haitian society as controlled by a small mulatto, Francophile élite would serve their political purposes admirably. Unwittingly, Leyburn – whose work was published in the Haitian press – was to provide the kind of evidence that François Duvalier would use to argue the case for ethno-cultural authenticity in Haitian politics.

The change in American attitudes to Haiti was almost complete by the late 1940s. The 'Good Neighbour Policy', scientific scrutiny and cultural relativism meant that Haitian culture and society had acquired a new respectability in the eyes of the United States. The best index to these dramatic changes in perspective was the revised approach to voodoo in this new phase. To the anthropologists, with their tape recorders and notebooks, voodoo was either studied as just another religion or treated as just another factor in Haitian society. By the late 1940s, the detachment of the scientist would be replaced by the enthusiasm of the convert. After World War II and the rise of black nationalism, 'the metaphysics of Vodoun' were 'discovered' according to Rémy Bastien.

> Deren, Rigaud and Jahn discoursed at length on the hierarchy of forces, on esoteric tradition, on cosmic and psychic orders. The evolution was complete: from diabolism and obscenity to ethics and philosophy.[13]

The difference between this new writing and earlier anthropological studies is the emphasis placed on Voodoo and racial essence. Earlier studies made the bizarre become ordinary. Haiti's new visitors now claimed that it was the extraordinary in Voodoo that made it the most seductive of all religions.

Maya Deren first visited Haiti in 1947 and her work on voodoo *Divine Horsemen: The Living God of Haiti* (1953) was her attempt to 'illuminate areas of Vodoun mythology with which the standard anthropological procedure had not concerned itself'.[14] Deren saw herself as an artist, marginalized and displaced within 'modern industrial culture'. She had been made an ethnic curiosity, subjected to 'the full "native" treatment', in American society. Consequently she approached Haiti as an 'artist–native' whose experience in the United States created a special bond with Haitians to whom she was 'not a foreigner at all, but a prodigal native daughter finally returned'. She insisted on a special affinity between herself and the Haitian peasant which allowed for communication on the subjective and emotional level. She trusted her artist's intuition more than the tools of scholarly research.

Deren's experience in Haiti was a journey from the periphery to the centre, from dispossession to ecstatic self-discovery. Deren, the artist–native, would have agreed with V. S. Naipaul's reflection on the taste for this kind of adventure as 'a writer's curiosity rather than an ethnographer's or journalist's'.[15] For Edmund

Wilson Haiti was the periphery. He had unshakeable faith that the United States was the centre. His secure centre was Deren's zone of marginalization. Displaced in the United States, she longed to find her centre in the unfamiliar and the strange. Indeed, Maya Deren is featured in Wilson's account of his stay in Haiti as a faintly ridiculous Haitian version of the phenomenon of the European 'gone native'.

She did not come to Haiti to observe but to be initiated. She scoffed at scholarly or scientific detachment as 'a projection of a dualism between spirit and matter, or the brain and the body'. The evidence that could be gained from the senses had traditionally been held in contempt. She felt that sensual experience was the only valid approach to Oriental and African cultures which were not based on the dualism of mind and body. It was precisely this thorough understanding of Haitian religion that, to her mind, eluded the trained anthropologist. Her work, she felt, would ultimately not only demonstrate the 'metaphysical structure of Haitian mythology' but also indicate the larger universal human pattern discernible to Haitian beliefs. In this regard, the work of Joseph Campbell was a shaping influence. Deren's account of Haitian voodoo was a plunge into the world of cosmic myth, of which only the artist was capable.

In his introduction to Alfred Metraux's study of voodoo in Haiti, Sidney Mintz observes that a 'good ethnographer . . . always recognizes that reality is, among other things, what people have learned to see'.[16] In general, the ethnography of the 1940s encouraged the United States to unlearn the traditional perception of Haitian society in terms of 'Otherness'. Difference was replaced by sameness. Hugh Cave's personal chronicle of a Haitian visit, entitled *Haiti, Highroad to Adventure* (1952) declares that 'Voodoo is religious philosophy' and the 'hounfor a sort of neighbourland church'.[17] The novel which was inspired by this fieldwork, entitled *The Cross on the Drum* (1958) is set in an island called St. Joseph, which closely resembles Haiti. As the title suggests, it deals with Haitian religion (the drum) and American religion (the cross). The bond between black houngan and white missionary is the main focus of the plot. The houngan is earnest and well intentioned like his American religious counterpart. The somewhat unlikely relationship between the two men is based on mutual respect. The missionary's words to the houngan almost echo the non-interventionist ideals of the post-Occupation years.

I respect your knowledge of native medicines. . . . I hope someday you'll share it with me. It's a knowledge handed down to you. . . . In a way it's also quite modern.[18]

In this phase of Haitian–American relations, it was not the strange or unfamiliar external appearance that mattered. The emphasis was on the normal and everyday processes that lay behind these disorienting phenomena. For about two decades a new discourse held at bay images of primeval menace that prevailed previously.

GOOD NEIGHBOURS AND RELUCTANT HOSTS: TWO HAITIAN VIEWS

This frontier was more than an example of cozy hypocrisy: It demonstrated all one needed to know about the morality of the Americas.

Paul Theroux

The liberal and open-minded treatment of Haiti by American commentators in the 1940s were strenuous exercises in cultural relativism as well as attempts to correct past distortions of Haiti's image. If American visitors to Haiti were motivated by guilt provoked by previous injustice, their Haitian hosts, still smarting from the humiliation of the American Occupation, were nervous about their new friends. Certainly, as far as the élite was concerned, Americans had taken an interest, albeit an earnest, high-minded one, in areas of popular culture normally held in contempt. Voodoo, folksongs and primitive art were considered too risky by a class anxious to demonstrate its intellectual achievements. James Leyburn is perceptive in his comment on the nervousness of the élite.

To associate for any length of time with the upper classes of Haitian society is to be aware of a deep unrest. . . . One discovers a large number of topics which had better not be discussed at all, for they bring a look of distress, wariness, or nervous tension to the face of one's host.[19]

One of these subjects is 'the opinion of the white world'. The hypersensitivity to comment from outside, indicates a deep insecurity in the face of the Other. For instance, none other than the famous peasant novelist himself, Philippe Thoby-Marcelin, would lament the fact that too much attention was being paid to primitive art while those who, because of their training, are incapable of 'le retour à la naïveté' were ignored.[20] Marcelin was typical of an entire class which believed that a cultivation of the intellect was the only means of achieving respectability.

For the most part, however, Haitians were relieved to see that their foreign guests had not come for cheap sensationalism but out of a desire to understand. Marcelin's wariness was often supplanted by an enthusiastic effusion among others who were overjoyed because of the good faith of Haiti's new visitors. Ludovic Rosemond, in his short work on *Haiti et les Etats Unis* (1945), describes the United States as one of the most generous and powerful nations in the world. He was particularly impressed by the new admiring attitude to Haitian culture. His book contains glowing tributes to those who praised Haiti. He refers to the 'learned comments of the eminent sociologists Herskovits, Locke, Dubois and Logan' as well as Mercer Cook's translations of Jacques Roumain and other indigenous writing into English. He includes Blair Niles 'among the most enthusiastic admirers of King Christophe' and Vandercook, who in *Black Majesty* had ranked 'the citadelle among the Wonders of the world'.[21] The American Occupation had forced Haiti out of its isolation. The naïveté and smugness of earlier time was now replaced by a spirit of watchful accommodation of the new American interest in Haitian culture.

Traditionally the American visitor to Haiti had been satirized in Haitian literature. The stereotype of the racist American braggart is one of the stock themes of writing during the American Occupation. The foreign invader or perhaps trespasser is usually ridiculed because of a tragi-comic combination of credulity and self-importance that drives him to hilarious misadventure in the Haitian countryside. Luc Grimard's 'Les deux couleuvres de Crackson' (1934), which gleefully redresses Haiti's self-esteem at the expense of a high-handed American, is typical of the use of this genre during the Occupation. However, the origins of this satire go back to the turn of the century. One of the earliest attempts to satirize the misguided Anglophone intruder can be found in the pages of *Le Nouvelliste* in March and April of 1902. It was written by Edmond Laforest and tells the story of an English anthropologist who comes on an illicit mission for Amerindian artefacts. 'Le Crâne de l'Indian Ciguäyo' is fully discussed by Beverley Ormerod who points to Laforest's 'sardonic West Indian streak in his mockery of Europeans'.[22] However, it is more precisely the Anglophone intruders who are ridiculed in this way. No French-speaking foreigner is ever humiliated in this grotesque fashion by Haitian writers.

Whereas Laforest mocked the duplicity of an English scholar and his Australian *protégé* – who has the outstandish name Mr. Cornbeef in this story – it is the American anthropologist who would feature in the post-Occupation period. Even as late as 1960, Jacques Stephen Alexis would include in his story 'Le sous-lieutenant enchanté' an American, ludicrously named Wheelbarrow, who poses as an archeologist interested in pre-columbian artefacts. However, in the 1940s, the American is not an impostor but trusting and respectful. His Haitian host is not maliciously gleeful because of his ignorance but helpful and understanding. This change in attitude is evident in every laborious detail of J. B. Cinéas' novel *L'Héritage Sacré* published in 1945.

The colour and ideological persuasion of the Haitian writer would be determining factors in the treatment of American scholars working on popular culture. Leyburn's theory of caste conflict in Haitian society seems to have been substantiated by the fierce tensions that divided blacks and mulattoes under Lescot's presidency (1941–45). Leyburn's notion of a caste society had such an impact at the time that extracts of *The Haitian People* were translated in the press. The pro-mulatto policies of Lescot were considered almost segregationist and his deep prejudice against peasant culture is certainly part of the reason why the Catholic Church attempted to eradicate Voodoo in its *Campagne anti-superstitieuse* waged in 1941–42. In such a situation, black Haitians defended popular culture and welcomed Americans who were interested in studying and promoting this area of Haitian culture. The social tensions within Haiti in the 1940s are clearly demonstrated by Alfred Métraux's conversation in November 1944 with Aimé Césaire, visiting Haiti at the time. While Césaire was warmly received by black intellectuals, the mulatto establishment remained deliberately indifferent. Césaire spoke to Métraux of the conflict between mulattoes and blacks and . . .

how his colour (had) determined the attitude of these groups towards him. Coldness of the Government, enthusiasm of the Blacks. Press campaign on his behalf organised by the blacks.[23]

It is precisely this internal conflict that determined the reception of American anthropologists. The work of Leyburn, Courlander and Herskovits was well received by 'noiriste' intellectuals as opposed to the anxious suspicion of the mulatto élite. Price-Mars reviewed *Life in a Haitian Valley* in 1937 in *La Relève* and praised the fairness and perceptiveness of Herskovits' account of peasant culture. He expressed his belief that this work had debunked the irritating image of the *Magic Island*.

> . . . je suis heureux que ce livre redresse les insanités et les colossales bêtises dont se repaît l'homme moyen qui se nourrit de Seabrook, de Craige, de Wirkus, et de Loederer. . . . Le moindre marine qui a passé quelque temps ici, entre 1915 et 1934, alléché par la fortune inespérée que Seabrook a tirée de la matière par sa *Magic Island*, s'est cru autorisé à vomir quelques ignominies sur la communauté haitienne.[24]
>
> (. . . I am happy that this book corrects the insanity and colossal stupidity consumed by the average man who feeds on Seabrook, Craige, Wirkus and Loederer. . . . The most insignificant marine who has spent a little time here, between 1915 and 1934, enticed by the unexpected fortune made from this material by Seabrook's *Magic Island*, felt authorised to vomit a few disgraceful remarks on Haitian society)

Herskovits was anything but 'le moindre marine' and the former's sensitivity to peasant culture is re-enacted by Cinéas in his novel.

L'Héritage Sacré, whose very title reveals an attitude of reverence to peasant culture, introduces an American Professor Phillips Benfield who has neither the exasperating smugness nor the outlandish name of Cornbeef or Wheelbarrow – even if 'Phillips' is an unlikely name. The American protagonist is obviously inspired by Herskovits whose name is mentioned in the foreword. Benfield, like Herskovits, has come to Haiti to write a book on 'la vie paysanne'. He is modest in his ambitions and promises to be 'le plus docile des élèves' (the most docile of pupils). Cinéas can hardly restrain the pedagogic impulse when he has Benfield leap to the defence of the Haitian people in language that could have been uttered by Price-Mars himself. He fiercely criticizes the 'Magic Island' school of writing on Haiti.

> Des conteurs à l'imagination trop riche, des mercantis de la plume, prennent plaisir à inventer des histories les plus étranges, les plus fantastiques, les plus invraisemblables sur le compte du peuple haitien. Malheureusement le public américain, trop crédule dans sa passion du 'sensationnel' accorde à ces fables ridicules le plus grand crédit.[25]

> (storytellers with overactive imaginations, mercenaries of the pen, take pleasure in inventing the strangest, the most fantastic, the most improbable stories at the expense of the Haitian people. Unfortunately the American public, too credulous in its passion for sensationalism places the greatest faith in these ridiculous tales)

Benfield goes on to declare that he, a white foreigner, lives alone in Haiti, and has never felt threatened. He has been treated with 'respect, consideration and friendship'. He remains eternally grateful for this warm welcome provided by a traditionally misunderstood people.

The self-consciously respectful American scholar is no less interesting than his Haitian interlocutor, who despite his interest in local culture is a very Gallic medical doctor. The suave, tolerant Dr. Justinien Melfort, whose solemn, understanding presence pervades the text, is always there to reassure his American companion. He compliments Benfield on his ability to fit in among the peasants, to become a 'pur Haiti-Thomas'. He, predictably, contrasts the American's knowledge of Haiti with the contempt of the élite for their people.

> Déjà le peu que vous savez de la campagne haïtienne est de beaucoup supérieur à la science de nos bourgeois prétentieux.[26]

> (Already the little you know of the Haitian countryside is greatly superior to the knowledge of our pretentious bourgeoisie.)

The relationship between Benfield and Melfort is almost a self-contained episode within the larger narrative and is essentially a literary re-enactment of an actual relationship that had developed between Haitian intellectuals who defended Voodoo and Americans who shared an interest in this subject.

In the novel these two learned and sophisticated gentlemen stand out against a background of rural simplicity and benign nature. Benfield is nothing like the marine or ex-marine in earlier fiction who competes with a Haitian for the attention of a local lady. The last such novel of amorous rivalry leading to a crime of passion was *Viejo* (1935). Anxious to be accepted by his Haitian host, Benfield is disarmingly restrained and sympathetic in his approach to Haitian society. This signifies the complete metamorphosis of the figure of the foreign intruder in Haitian writing. The fact that Benfield is not a Francophone does not go unnoticed. This is a gentle mockery of his nasal voice and his poor French in a narrative that is bristling with the high-minded erudition of Melfort – 'Antée renaît toujours à la vie, au contact de la mater alma' (Anteus come back to life through contact with the alma mater). The dialogue between the two men is filled with the anglicized or incorrect French of Benfield but a passion for science unites the two men.

> L'accent nasillard, les impropriétés de termes, les singularités syntaxiques assaisonnaient les discours du Professeur américain Phillips Benfield de délices imprévues et de saveur inédite. Pourtant, son compagnon et interlocuteur, le Dr. Justinien Melfort, l'écoutait sans sourire, avec sérieux, indifférent à ses fautes de français. . . . La passion de la science les avait cuirassés d'indulgence l'un pour l'autre. Ils voulaient se comprendre; . . . Le principal, c'était de s'entendre et ils s'entendaient merveilleusement.[27]

> (The nasal accent, incorrect expressions, syntactic peculiarities flavoured the speech of the American Professor Phillips Benfield with unexpected delights and unusual flavours. However, his companion and interlocutor, Dr. Justinien Melfort, listened to him without smiling, serious, indifferent to his flawed French. . . . The love for science had armed them with indulgence for each other. They wanted to understand each other; . . . the important thing was to understand each other and they did so marvellously.)

In the 1940s an older and wiser American comes courting and his overtures are met with a benign tolerance.

In this best of all possible worlds, the natives are not restless and the intruder is benign. A grave piety surrounds the encounter between American scholar anxious to ennoble what he observes and the latinate expansiveness of his Haitian host. This cross-cultural coziness is both unconvincing and contrived. It seems particularly unreal since the attitudes of some Haitians were becoming increasingly hostile by 1945, when the novel was published.[28] Perhaps the ostentatious hospitality of Melfort and the excessive reverence of Benfield do in themselves betray the uneasiness of Cinéas in treating this encounter. By the mid 1940s Haitian peasants were not inoffensive souls having fun in the woods but found themselves dispossessed because of the excesses of Lescot's pro-American policy. Official relations between Lescot's government and the United States were good in the early 1940s. Evidence of this can be seen in the creation of a Haitian–American Institute in Port-au-Prince. Haiti also declared war on Japan after the bombing of Pearl Harbor. It was precisely Lescot's enthusiastic role in the American war effort that would increase hostility to the United States and bring about Lescot's downfall.

Lescot's relationship with the United States came under increasing attack in the early 1940s because of the joint venture of a North American company and the Haitian government to produce in Haiti rubber and sisal to help America in the war against Japan. SHADA (the Haitian American Society for Development of Agriculture) undertook to grow in Haiti a special plant that could be used in the manufacture of rubber in the United States. In order to grow this plant on a large scale, peasant lands were expropriated and their traditional crops destroyed. The plight of Haiti's peasantry was an important factor in the growth of anti-Lescot Opposition in Haiti. The movement that finally drove Lescot into exile in 1946 was led by a generation of younger Haitians who resented the fact that even after the Occupation, the United States continued to intervene in Haiti's internal affairs.

What came to be known as the 'generation of '46' was made up of young Haitians who, in spite of not experiencing the American Occupation, had been deeply influenced by Jacques Roumain's ideas. Leftist ideology, political activism, the revolutionary role of the writer were all part of the Roumain legacy. Roumain's interest in peasant culture was evident in his founding of the *Bureau d'Ethnologie* in 1941 with Price-Mars as director. Roumain had also attacked the Catholic Church for its campaign to eradicate Voodoo in the Haitian countryside. Consequently his reputation as a defender of the Haitian people and his international stature meant that he was idolized by the Haitian youth at the time. René Depestre, one of the leading figures in the anti-Lescot movement of 1946, spoke of Roumain's role in the general political radicalism of the times. Through Roumain, a whole new world was opened in the 1940s. Also young Haitians were exposed to the visits of a number of foreign writers and intellectuals at this time.

> . . . on dècouvrait alors l'existence des poèmes de Lorca et de Machado, les romans de Gorki, la peinture de Picasso, les vers de Paul Eluard, Roumain, Césaire, Langston Hughes et Vladimir Maiakovsky! Sons oublier les voix majeures de Nicolas Guillen, Pablo Neruda, César Vallejo. Une fois, un matin de 1942, nous vîmes entrer Nicolas Guillen dans notre classe du lycée Pétion, en compagnie de Jacques Roumain. Un nouveau monde naissait sous nos yeux. . . . Nous eûmes, un soir, un ciné Paramount, la révélaiton d'Alejo Carpentier! . . . Césaire nous fit des conferences extraordinaires sur Rimbaud et Lautréamont . . . André Breton . . . lors de ses conférences, au cinéma Rex de Port-au-Prince . . . lâchait des formules qui étaient comme des flèches du feu à l'arc des jeunes gens que nous étions cette année-la.[29]

> (. . . we then discovered the existence of the poems of Lorca and Machado, the novels of Gorki, the painting of Picasso, the verses of Paul Eluard, Roumain, Césaire, Langston Hughes and Vladimir Maiakovsky! Not to mention the powerful voices of Nicolas Guillen, Pablo Neruda, César Vallejo. One morning in 1942, we saw Nicolas Guillen enter our class in the lycée Pétion, accompanied by Jacques Roumain. A new world was born before our eyes. . . . We had, one evening, at the Paramount cinema, the revelations of Alejo Carpentier! . . . Césaire gave extraordinary lectures on Rimbaud and Lautréamont . . . André Breton, at his lectures in the Rex cinema in Port-au-Prince . . . unleashed ideas which were like arrows of fire in the bows of we the young generation in that year.)

Visitors like Breton, Césaire and Carpentier would have a greater and quite different impact on the generation than Herskovits,

Courlander and Leyburn. These new literary radicals were invited by Pierre Mabille and the Institut Français – not the Haitian–American Institute. The dispossession of the peasantry, the exploitative presence of SHADA and the intrusion of multinationals like Standard Fruit became targets for the explosive energies of Depestre and his colleagues. At the end of World War II a desire for change was everywhere apparent. In Haiti dissatisfaction with Lescot intensified and in 1946 this group of young leftist students led the strike that swept Lescot from power.

The image that this generation promoted was that of the precocious 'enfant terrible', irreverent, provocative and idealistic. This image is defined by Depestre himself in the collection of poetry entitled *Etincelles* (1945). He presents himself in these terms:

> Me voici
> poète
> adolescent
> poursuivant un rêve immense d'amour et de liberté.[30]
>
> (Here I am
> poet
> adolescent
> in pursuit of a great dream of love and freedom.)

In contrast to this image of the reckless, youthful subversive, the figure of the corpulent, grasping American businessman had been poignantly fixed in Haitian literature by Jacques Roumain in *Gouverneurs de la rosée* (1944). In this novel the Haitian protagonist who migrates to Cuba to cut cane, describes the American who owned the plantation not as a worthy Professor Benfield but as sadistic Mister Wilson 'assis dans le jardin de la belle maison sous un parasol' (sitting in the garden of his beautiful house under an umbrella). He sits in protected luxury while hundreds of 'peones' slave under the hot sun in his plantation.

The change in government in 1946 signified the triumph of youthful idealism but more practically a victory for the black Haitian middle class, which Leyburn had chosen to ignore in his analysis of Haitian society. Leyburn's prediction that in 'the near future it is safe to say that there will be no more black non-élite presidents'[31] was hopelessly wrong. Dumarsais Estimé's election as president of Haiti in August 1946 put an end to the blindly pro-American policies of the mulatto élite and placed on centre stage two groups who were suspicious of American intentions – leftist radicals and moderate black nationalists. The late 1940s in Haiti were marked by Marxist rhetoric, black nationalism and the weakening of mulatto hegemony. Estimé's timidity may have been his undoing as he was overthrown in 1950. The military general who took his place, Paul Magloire, made a last desperate bid to reinstate the conservative mulatto élite and their pro-American attitudes. Magloire even appeared on the cover of *Time* magazine but in 1956 he followed Estimé into exile. The way was open for Estimé's less timid supporters, among whom was the shrewd and inscrutable François Duvalier, who came to power in 1957.

The attack on the United States' indirect intervention in Haiti by young Marxist radicals grew more intense in the wake of the events of 1946. They supported Estimé's government as the defender of the peasantry and the working class. There were to be seriously disappointed by Estimé's hesitancy and his eventual anti-communist position. Estimé rid himself of these student radicals by offering the leaders of the movement scholarships to study abroad. Both René Depestre and Jacques Stephen Alexis, who were responsible for a vigorous anti-Americanism in Haitian literature, were destined to spend the next decade in Europe because of Estimé's calculating generosity. For both of these writers the events of 1946 were indelible memories and they would spend the rest of their lives hoping that their imaginations could once again detonate the collective 'prise de conscience' necessary for revolutionary change.

Depestre's poetry of the early 1950s is marked by a disappointing Stalinism and a commitment to denounce American imperialism globally. *Végétation de clarté* (Luminous growths), which appeared in 1951, and *Traduit du grand large* (Translated across the waters) in 1952 are chronicles of Depestre's vagrancy at the time as well as a denunciation of Estimé and other reactionary, corrupt politicians in Haiti and Latin America. In Depestre's poetic world view Yankee machinations are everywhere apparent and Marxism will bring salvation. These are not particularly Haitian poems but anonymously international in tone and predictably Manichean in their division of the world into malevolent Imperialists and the noble oppressed.

While Depestre's early poetic fulminations against the fraudulence and hypocrisy of the Haitian establishment had grown into bland political propaganda, his contemporary Jacques Stéphen Alexis would create fictional works that record persuasively the growing distrust of American manipulations of the Haitian situation. His novels are more historically oriented than those of his precursor Jacques Roumain but continue Roumain's lyrical evocations of the world of impoverished Haitians and his inexhaustible faith in their capacity to survive. In Alexis' early fiction the short-lived satire of Mr. Wilson, Roumain's caricature of American Imperialism, is expanded to become a sustained, caustic depiction of the American presence in Haiti and the élite's capacity to succumb to its blandishments. If André Breton had profoundly influenced the young Depestre, it was Alejo Carpentier whose theories of 'Marvellous Realism' had marked Alexis. However, Alexis was not only concerned with depicting the mythical and imaginative world-view of the peasant in his work, he had an equally intense interest in social and political satire. To this extent he brought to the Haitian novel a political focus and an imaginative scale, a 'conciliation de l'imaginaire et du réel' that one normally associates with Latin American fiction.

Alexis' first novel, *Compère Général Soleil*, was published in 1955, one year after his return to Haiti. It is a work of epic proportions in which a didactic impulse is often shrilly apparent. It examines the events of 1936 and 1937 in Haiti and in particular the massacre of Haitian migrant workers in Dominican Republic through the experiences of the protagonist Hilarion who is ensnared in a world of privation and wretchedness. The novel is constructed in terms of a series of antithetical images that govern plot, characterization and landscape. Space and time are broken into images of ascent and fall, darkness and light, estrangement and solidarity, illumination and blindness.[32] This system of binary opposites also applies to the politics of the novel as characters in the novel are rigidly divided into the admirable downtrodden as opposed to the despicable wealthy bourgeoisie. It is through the latter that America's presence in Haiti is criticized. Alexis is unrelenting in his portrayal of the bourgeois Haitian politician as a tool of American imperialism – 'l'homme des villes est esclave des Américains' (the city dweller is the slave of the Americans) and in particular the ingratiating politician Jérôme Paturault who epitomizes the spineless, scheming mulatto who finally gets a diplomatic post in 'la métropole du dollar'. At an extravagant party organized by Paturault and his wife, the sounds of the 'Lambeth Walk' are used to drown the cries of anger and hunger from the crowd of impoverished Haitian workers.[33]

The caricature of the American presence in Haiti is fierce and sustained. It is invariably associated with images of oppressive weight and casual brutality. The American automobile symbolizes the crushing weight of Imperialism on the frail body of Haiti or the roar of self-satisfaction against the small cries of Haitian higglers.

> . . . des voitures américaines qui, comme d'énormes crapauds, se promènent sur le corps de la pauvre Haiti. (p. 34)

> (. . . American cars which, like huge toads, strut across the body of poor Haiti)

> . . . à l'heure où les marchands ambulants lancent dans les rues fraîches leurs premiers cris. . . . Les moteurs des grosses voitures américaines démarrèrent, rugissants . . . (p. 192)

> (. . . at the time when the higglers' first cries fill the innocence of the streets. . . . The motors of huge American cars roared into life . . .)

Along with the image of blind material power can be found the ever-present drunk Marine who mindlessly inflicts suffering on the poor and unfortunate. A group of Marines force an emaciated female beggar to dance on all fours and pick up an American dollar with her mouth (p. 203). An invasion of drunken sailors simply intensifies the picture of arrogant brutishness.

> Brilliant nasillardement des rengaines, on dirait que ces derniers avaient décidé de vider le pays de tout le rhum qu'il pouvait produire. . . . Les seigneurs du dollar foulaient le pavé en maîtres, se vautraient dans les caniveaux, hurlaient, grimpaient aux réverbères, faisaient mille et une excentricités.
>
> (p. 227)

> (From their noisy, nasal singing, one felt that the latter had decided to empty the country of all the rum it could produce. . . . These masters of the dollar strutted across the pavement as

if they owned it, wallowed in the gutters, shouted, climbed the lamp-posts, did a thousand and one absurdities)

The resentment is real but not simply racist. The Americans are ridiculed in Alexis' first novel but they are seen as the most recent invasion of foreigners, the new conquistadors, who take advantage of Haiti 'la grande invasion des nouveaux vandales, les Américains'. Alexis in *Compère Général Soleil* had begun to see Haitian history in terms of cycles of greed and conquest which would be a consistent motif in all his writing.

Les arbres musiciens (1957) is in some ways even more polemical and didactic than Alexis' earlier work. The historical context of this work is the Catholic Church's campaign to eradicate Voodoo (la campagne anti-superstitieuse) and the expropriation of land from the Haitian peasantry by SHADA. In a novel which is politically digressive, Alexis occasionally stops the story abruptly to include accounts of events which are treated in laborious detail. The plot of the novel turns on the conflict between those who oppress Haiti – the Church, the Government, the United States – and the resistance of those who belong to the luxuriant hinterland of the forest. The spectacular wilderness of the Haitian forest has sheltered and protected those who must now face the aggression of ruthless or misguided individuals who wish to undermine its values and its musical voice in order to exploit its resources. Collusion between the United States and the Catholic Church in order to wage war on the Haitian peasantry is dramatized in a conspiratorial meeting between American Ambassador and the Catholic Archbishop. The latter makes the following sinister offer

> La S.H.A.D.A., quoi qu'en dise le gouvernement haitien, ne va pas avoir la tâche facile . . . Nous projetons une campagne anti-superstitieuse . . . Nous pourrions peut-être unir nos forces?[34]
>
> (S.H.A.D.A., whatever the government says, is not going to have an easy job. . . . We plan an anti-superstition campaign. . . . We could perhaps join forces?)

Since Voodoo would be an obstacle to the exploitation of peasant land, the Church's campaign could undermine resistance to allow the work of SHADA to proceed. As the American Ambassador puts it . . . 'le goupillon doit préceder le tracteur . . .' (the aspergillum must precede the tractor).

Alexis, like most of his generation, saw the blood-stained hands of American imperialism in every aspect of Haitian life. He reserves his most bitter satire for the insecure opportunists of Port-au-Prince who are only too anxious to yield to American values. He ridicules those Haitians who go off to American universities and return as qualified experts in a dismayingly short period of time. They are seen as a new Zoological species, able to metamorphose more quickly than a chameleon, with the characteristic oiled hair, short pipe, chewing gum and American jargon. 'Homo Americanus' was created in certain American universities and then unleashed on Haitian society.

Les plus grandes couveuses de 'master of' étaient les universités de Columbia, de Yale. La production se faisait électriquement . . .
– A columbia, on devient M.A. (comprenez Master in Art) en deux mois et demi . . .
– Tu parles! J'ai été reçu Master of Science de Fisk University en soixante cinq jours et quart!
– Et moi Master in Art, Bachelor of Technology de Yale, le tout en deux mois juste . . .[35]

(The biggest hatcheries for 'Master of' were the universities of Columbia, Fisk and Yale. They were produced by electricity . . .
– At Columbia, you become M.A. (that is Master in Art) in two and a half months . . .
– Listen to this! I graduated with a Master of Science from Fisk University in sixty five and a quarter days!
– And I Master in Art, Bachelor of Technology from Yale, all in just two months . . .)

Alexis can scarcely conceal his revulsion as he caricatures Haitians who, perhaps for the first time in Haitian literature, dress and speak like Americans. His desperate hope was that the powerful voice of the forest would overwhelm the sounds of Well! O.K.! 'Hello, guys!' (p. 159). However, the persistent image in his novels is that of Haiti prostituted to the Americans. This becomes the central motif in *L'espace d'un cillement* (1959) in which the brothel 'Sensation Bar' serves as a symbol of Haiti – a 'magic island' devoted to entertainment of debauched Americans.

Alexis' interest in the United States drove him to write a play entitled *Les dollars* which was set in Florida. In this unpublished text, he looked at the black and white working class very much in the manner of Roumain's analysis of the American proletariat deliberately divided and therefore undermined by the white establishment. The Folksner household is a microcosm of the exploitative American establishment. For instance a South American Ambassador is a family friend and he protects their interests in Latin America. This play indicates Alexis' sympathies for the disenfranchised of whatever colour, whether white dockworker or black gardener. The generosity of Alexis' literary imagination is most apparent in a short story that appeared a year before his death – 'Le sous lieutenant enchanté'.

This short story has many antecedents in Haitian literature. Edmond Laforest, Luc Grimard and J.-B. Cinéas had all treated the theme of the Anglophone intruder who comes, with sometimes benign and sometimes sinister motives, to seek his fortune in the Haitian heartland. Alexis' protagonist has come to Haiti seeking Amerindian treasure in 1914. He has an outlandish name, Lieutenant Wheelbarrow, and has grown up in the southern United States. However, Alexis' anti-American impulses are restrained in this story since he is interested in Wheelbarrow's inability to fit into the parochial world of a small Southern town and his capacity to accommodate the startlingly unfamiliar world of Haiti.

Wheelbarrow – 'contradictoire, idéaliste généreux' – finds himself distracted from his original materialistic quest by a seductive Amerindian female who is the spirit of the Haitian interior. He realizes his error in trespassing on Haiti's ancestral space and renounces his past to joint this mysterious female in the miraculous, primeval heartland. Wheelbarrow's initiation by this tutelary goddess illustrates two of Alexis' concerns – his belief in the basic humanity of all men and in the overwhelming power of Haiti's enduring heartland. Wheelbarrow's diary records his ecstatic fusion with the supernatural in the warmth of a subterranean grotto. He achieves that supreme wisdom which synthesizes all things and unites all opposites . . . 'ce point de savoir humain où l'on participe à toute respiration, à toute vibration de la matière vivante . . .'[36] (that point in human wisdom where you are a part of all the throbbing vibration of living matter). Alexis' fictional world begins with images of contradictions and antithesis in *Compère Général Soleil* and ends with a vision of the integrating force of a world of ceaseless renewal. Alexis would have agreed with Alejo Carpentier that Haiti represented the essential American frontier, a 'magical crossroads' of cultures. Carpentier asked in 1948

> ... By virtue of the virginity of its landscape; of the formation, ontology and magic presence of the Indian and the black man; of the creative cross-fertilisation that was produced. ... What is the whole history of America but a chronicle of 'marvellous realism'?[37]

Wheelbarrow discovers, in his immersion in a world of sensation, the 'Kingdom of this World' – that is his true American heritage. His experience is a vital part of New World history. He transcends the Old World prejudices that oppose pure and impure, developed and undeveloped, strong and weak. Not surprisingly, he is shot by his fellow Americans for consorting with the enemy, during the Occupation which was justified in the name of material progress and moral purity.

'Les sous-lieutenant enchanté' is ultimately a persuasive critique of power, domination and bourgeois notions of individuality. Alexis, in his last work, seems to be attempting nothing less than a redefinition of the Haitian subject. Gone are the rivalry and insecurity that generated images of the self-regarding 'nègre' or the affected classical scholar. The Haitian subject, in Alexis' fiction, is characterized by resilience, suppleness and secretiveness. What seems uppermost in Alexis' mind is the creative incompleteness of this subject which allows it to absorb or combine with any alien presence. Alexis' fictional discourse turns on the relationship between inhibiting notions of power and the promise of its subversion. By 1960 Alexis demonstrated that rare capacity that allowed him to transcend the imaginative constraints that had fixed the Haitian subject and the American 'Other' in a relationship built on suspicion and uneasiness. However, in the 1960s, Duvalierism would mean a revival of an earlier discourse that marginalized Haiti and once more fix Haitian–American relations in terms of moral contempt and cultural incompatibility.

5
The Art of Darkness: Writing in the Duvalier Years

HAITI'S BLACK COMEDY

> We were cut off from the comprehension of our surroundings; we glided past like phantoms, wondering and secretly appalled, as sane men would be before an enthusiastic outbreak in a madhouse.
>
> Joseph Conrad, *Heart of Darkness*

Just as Joseph Conrad had earlier supplied the dominant images of Africa in the European imagination, in the 1960s Graham Greene performed the same dubious service for Haiti in the Western imagination. The puritanical crusader immersed in sensual darkness; the unspeakable kingdom of the night; a static, timeless world of absence – these durable and influential images establish an imaginative quarantine around Africa and Haiti in Conrad's *Heart of Darkness* (1899) and Greene's *The Comedians* (1966). There is no American equivalent to Greene's novel about Haiti, no work that has spawned so many different versions, rewritings or interpretations of itself. American attitudes to Haiti from the 1960s onwards are marked by the singular influence of *The Comedians* and its debt to Conrad's earlier imaginative fixing of Africa. Christopher Miller's comment on the significance of *Heart of Darkness* as the beginning of a special tradition of 'Africanist discourse' is pertinent.

> The initial perception of a discourse as 'Africanist' would perhaps not be possible without the perspective afforded by reading Conrad's *Heart of Darkness*, the strongest of all Africanist texts ... it defines the condition of possibility of Africanist discourse.[1]

Heart of Darkness, that defining moment in European narrative, becomes the master text for Greene whose novel *The Comedians* defines an imaginative discourse, a fictional orthodoxy, that determines Haiti's visibility under the rule of François Duvalier.

The literary relationship between Conrad and Greene illustrates two concerns that are of great importance to us. Firstly, it is a perfect example of what Edward Said in his discussion of Orientalism called a 'textual attitude' – that is the capacity of narrative to so condition our view of a particular subject that its images acquire a greater authority than reality itself. Indeed political, historical and cultural reality will be interpreted or even distorted to conform with the demands of an imaginative discourse. Conrad made Africa into a perversely evocative 'sign', a textually produced 'Other' because of the hypnotic power of his depiction of Africa as the 'heart of an impenetrable/barren/conquering darkness'. Writing about Africa or any other blank space or 'heart of darkness' inevitably undergoes the shaping influence of Conrad's text. The capacity for endless suggestiveness in Conrad's discourse must, to some extent, be related to the fact that even though the reference in his text is obviously Africa it is never specifically named. What Miller astutely observes as a 'repression of the referent' in Conrad's text means that the 'blank space' for which Marlow had a 'hankering' since his boyhood could now be filled in by any novelist or travel writer with an equally intense desire to journey into the world of the unexplored or the outlandish. For instance, V. S. Naipaul in his fascination with 'blank spaces' on the map, admits to feeling that wherever he goes Conrad has preceded him:

> Conrad . . . had been everywhere before me. Not as a man with a cause, but a man offering . . . a vision of the world's half-made societies as places which continuously made and unmade themselves . . . Conrad's value to me is that he is someone who sixty to seventy years ago meditated on my world, a world I recognize today.[2]

Although, admittedly less culturally complacent than Conrad, Naipaul is one of the modern novelists cum travel writers who share Marlow's 'fascination of the abomination'. In his scrutiny of the 'Conradian dark places of the earth' Naipaul makes the significant link between Zaire and Haiti in his essay 'Mobutu and the Nihilism of Africa'.[3] This relationship is even more fully explored by Graham Greene who is, in many ways, quite different from the world-weary displaced ex-colonial from Trinidad, but with whom he shares an imaginative submissiveness to Conrad's textual discourse.

Conrad's master text also made Africa intelligible for Greene. We can almost imagine Greene, to use Michel Foucault's image, as a latter-day Quixote whose early reading plays a decisive role in his deciphering of the world. Like Cervantes' misguided hero, he felt the need 'to remain faithful to the book' that formed his perception of Africa.[4] It is this fidelity that illustrates the second and related concern that is of importance to us. The intertextual relationship that is discernible in the link between *Heart of Darkness* and Greene's early travel writing on Liberia – *Journey without Maps* (1936). The difference between novel writing and the travel writing of the novelist is not really all that great. The novelist travels for the thrill of alien space. He is always in search of that salutary displacement, that surprising 'Otherness' which is for him an end in itself. Unlike the journalist or anthropologist who is expected to stay long enough to be able to understand and explain, the travelling novelist leaves when the adventure is over and perhaps when understanding is about to begin. Consequently fiction and travel writing are both adventures into the unknown which are aimed not at reducing 'Otherness' but at its aesthetic exploitation. *Heart of Darkness* and *Journey without Maps* are linked by this particular element in their narrative strategies. Their relationship seems to illustrate Kristeva's view of the text 'as a mosaic of quotations' since Greene's text 'absorbs and transforms' Conrad's discourse.

For both Conrad and Greene the underdeveloped world is an imaginative source of raw materials. Africa and other similar 'blank spaces' because they are conceived as static and outside of time allow for a journey back in time to man and society at an earlier stage of development. Greene shares with Conrad the perception of Africa as that special zone, a moral testing-ground, which allows the traveller the chance of finding

> ... the 'heart of darkness' ... one's place in time, based on a knowledge not only of one's present but of the past from which one has emerged.[5]

Alienation from the excessive 'cerebration' of Europe makes Greene long for 'a quality of darkness' in order 'to discover if one can, from what we have come, to recall at which point we went astray'.[6] *Journey without Maps* is a Baudelairean voyage of damnation, a puritanical fascination with Fallenness and decay, where the customary emblems of the civilized world – books, pianos and gramophone records – rot and buckle. This unspeakable, barbaric, timeless Africa has an inexhaustible fascination for Greene. However, unlike an earlier voyager Arthur Rimbaud, he suffers from a failure of nerve . . . 'it isn't that one wants to stay in Africa: I have no yearning for a mindless sensuality'.[7]

'Le vraisemblable' or what could be accepted as true with reference to Africa had been textually ordained by Conrad's short novel. In both Greene and Conrad the journey into the primitive world is simultaneously a journey into the heart of man. Greene confesses that in spite of the topography, Africa was 'not a particular place, but a shape . . . that of the human heart'. Conrad's Marlow may have been somewhat more horrified than Greene at his 'remote kinship with this wild and passionate uproar'. Nevertheless, Greene's representation of Africa is no less repulsive. Indeed, he admits to being drawn to the squalor, to the seductive appeal of 'the dirt, the disease, the barbarity and the familiarity of Africa'. Perhaps for Greene the kinship is less 'remote' because he seems to have a sense of the Jungian archetypes that govern all human behaviour. For him the primeval bush and the screaming savage are still perceptible in the civilized world. But even if Africa is not Europe's nightmare, a stark dichotomy still governs its literary representation. It is the world of arrested development, of simplified emotions, of life lived 'below the level of the cerebral'. The reductionist imagery of Conrad's discourse is never too far away.

Greene wrote in a less innocent time than Conrad. The imminence of World War II reminds Greene that Europe was capable of a savagery not unlike that found in Africa. However, this perception of exhausted, troubled Europe does not diminish the Conradian resonance of the representation of Africa's 'Otherness'. In his search for a lost innocence Greene's journey took the imaginative route that had been mapped by Conrad's *Heart of Darkness*. At the end of his travelogue, Greene, while protesting that 'the heart of darkness was common to' both Africa and Europe, is ready to return to civilization. The salutary derangement is over but the land and its people remain captives of Greene's rewriting of Conrad's narrative. It is a discourse that marginalizes those 'blank spaces' in images of transgression, irresponsibility and ultimately insanity. Like the madhouse, Africa permits the unspeakable potential of man to erupt. Leavis gives the appropriate emphasis to this aspect of Conrad's *Heart of Darkness*

> Ordinary greed, stupidity, and moral squalor are made to look like behaviour in a lunatic asylum against the vast and oppressive mystery of the surroundings, rendered potently in terms of sensation.[8]

Greene's representation of Haiti in the 1960s is an extension of the Conradian discourse that permeates his earlier African travelogue.

As we have seen, Haiti, like Africa, had been fixed 'textually' since the nineteenth century as a literary 'sign', inexhaustively suggestive of mystery and carnality. Spenser St. John's account of 'The Black Republic' (1884) sent a shudder of disgust through the minds of his Victorian readership. The same disturbing pleasure awaited Greene's readers in the 1960s. St. John's account of Haiti was set at the time of the presidency or rather monarchy of Faustin Souloque, which is as depressing a moment in Haitian political history as the presidency of Duvalier. At both times, international opinion was convinced that Haiti had slipped back into barbarity and wretchedness. In the early 1960s, Duvalier's ruthlessness as a politician was becoming more apparent as he gradually and brutally silenced all opposition or potential sources of opposition to his rule. It was a time of attempted invasions, refugees seeking asylum in foreign embassies, and the United States, outmanoeuvred by Duvalier, reopening diplomatic relations with Haiti because it represented a bulwark against Cuban-inspired subversion in the Caribbean. This forms the general background to Greene's novel *The Comedians*.

The Comedians is described by Molly Mahood as 'one of the most *engagés* books of our time' and 'a genuine novel about the Third World'.[9] There is no doubting the truth of many of the events included in this work as Greene himself explains in the letter that serves as an introduction to the novel. One could also say that a small theme in the work is the relationship between the United States and Haiti. Greene does depict American attitudes which range from the faintly absurd naiveté of the Smiths who plan to open, in a land obsessed with the disfigurement and torture of human flesh, a vegetarian centre 'which one day would remove acidity and passion from the Haitian character' to the corpulent anti-communist Schuyler Wilson who cynically supports Duvalier because he keeps the red peril in the Caribbean at bay. To this extent, the political thrust of the novel is shrewd and perceptive. However, there is dismaying evidence of Greene's early fascination with the *Heart of Darkness* in this novel. *The Comedians* is also about one of these 'blank spaces' on the map, engulfed in an interminable night, akin to that experienced by Conrad's Marlow.

The belief that Haiti had simply lapsed into savagery in the 1960s had acquired great currency. For instance, in 1966, the very year in which Greene's novel appeared, Francis Huxley published his popular Haitian travelogue *The Invisibles*. Huxley, whose interest was in mental illness, went in search of examples of abnormal psychology and behaviour. He would inevitably discover what he was determined to find. His summary of Haitian society is a classic example of the marginalizing discourse that condemns Haiti to 'Otherness'.

> Notorious for its Voodoo and its zombis . . . its poverty is disgusting, its politics horrible, its black magic a matter of fantasy.[10]

Conrad's 'lunatic asylum' had once more been located. Greene, since his experience of primordial darkness in Liberia, had gone on to suffer articulately in Mexico. The moral corruption and physical discomfort of this 1930s journey are apparent in the text of *The Lawless Roads* (1939). By the time he gets to Haiti, Greene is a seasoned campaigner. The seediness of Liberia and the squalor of Mexico acquire a shrill intensity in Haiti, the most damned of Greene's moral landscapes.

It is sometimes difficult to share Mahood's view of the novel as simply politically engagé. This would suggest a more robust, heroic narrative but Greene has a taste for human weakness. He is far more attracted to betrayal, injustice and human failure than the nobility and the goodness of man. This curious fatalism that seems ever present in Greene achieves a gloomy oppressiveness in *The Comedians*. The politics of the novel are simply the superficial configuration. Duvalier's diabolical presence and malevolent

'Tonton Macoutes' are more a product of Catholic theology than political reality. The Conradian discourse, which generated images in Liberia of roads swallowed up by the night, now focuses unflinchingly on an impenetrable and unrelieved darkness.

The key to the tragic landscape of Haiti is provided in Greene's short introduction.

> Poor Haiti and the character of Doctor Duvalier's rule are not invented, the latter not even blackened for dramatic effect. Impossible to deepen that night.[11]

Conrad's all-encompassing darkness is now located in Haiti. This dark is a defining characteristic, an ineradicable atmosphere that shapes Greene's vision of Haiti. The textual 'vraisemblance' of Conrad's African novella now provides Greene with what would be accepted as a credible depiction of Haiti under Duvalier's rule. As Leavis would say, 'ordinary political injustice and moral squalor are made to look like behaviour in a lunatic asylum' because of the oppressive, all-encompassing darkness within which Greene's comedians act out their tragic roles. The real world has been left behind for a stranger place where 'only the nightmares are real'. The old postcards of his hotel, which the main protagonist Brown displays at the beginning, are 'printed in bright vulgar colours' but now gone for ever. Haiti is entombed in darkness. There are the arbitrary black-outs. The Tonton Macoutes wear 'dark glasses and call on their victims after dark'. The town even in daylight is in deep shadow because of the looming mass of Kenscoff. The night is everywhere and men must get accustomed to seeing in the dark. The Tonton Macoutes leave a trail of blackness in their wake.

> In the public park the musical fountain stood black, waterless, unplaying . . . we passed the blackened beams of the house the Tontons had destroyed.[12]

As if to enhance the terror of the dark, there is reckless drumming in the night and an ever-present thunderstorm threatens over the surrounding mountains.

The creatures who inhabit this subterranean dark are luridly portrayed. Greene's narrator sees manifestations of the diabolical at every turn. His mother's lover Marcel, a black man, kneeling at her bedside looked like 'some negro-priest at an obscene rite'. Equally startling is the metamorphosis of his friend Dr. Magiot who 'looked like a sorcerer exorcizing death' crouched over the body in Brown's hotel. The shadows are more substantial than the objects that cast them and reality itself is unstable. Sisal drying can look like 'tresses of blonde hair . . . ripped from the skulls of women buried below'. Lurid and melodramatic, Greene's vision of Haiti does not benefit from the cool ironic focus of his better fiction. Indeed this darkness is presided over by the gaze of Duvalier who stares down from his poster 'as though at a body ready for dissection'. Haiti is reduced in the narrative to a world of deformed flesh '- beggars, beggars, everywhere'. It is a pitiable and unlovely world like the Congo leprosarium of *A Burnt-Out Case* (1961). Deformed humanity, both physical and moral, scuttle about the landscape. Brown arrives in Haiti and a legless man sits under the customs counter 'like a rabbit in a hutch, miming in silence'. Brown has at one point to fight his way through 'a typical scene at the Post Office' in which he encounters 'a stiff human stump like a piece of hard rubber'. The Haitian night is represented as a black body 'out of breath, supine, its pulse labouring'. The collective disfigurement is kept in the foreground of the narrative because of the limping Joseph, Brown's servant at the hotel. This unrelieved spectacle of human debasement seems to echo the primitive brutality of Conrad's world. Marlow sees before him what he calls 'raw matter' arranged in states of abjection.

> Black shapes crouched, lay, sat between the trees leaning against the trunks, clinging to the earth, . . . in all the attitudes of pain, abandonment, and despair.[13]

For Greene in the 1960s, the discourse remains essentially unchanged.

In all this, there stands the white stone statue of Columbus in whose shadow Brown and Martha have their joyless, clandestine meetings. 'A stone Columbus' who is always 'staring at the sea' has an important symbolic resonance in the text. A petrified white figure, who has turned his back on the darkness, almost seems to epitomize the sense of human failure Greene evokes in Haiti. Cast away and marginalized in a world he once discovered but now controlled by malevolent blacks, he symbolizes the absurdity of his adventure. A tragic Promethean figure, he is chained for ever to this squalor that he inaugurated. Haiti's comedy has historic dimensions in Greene's imagination. Brown, going to seed in this outlandish place, is simply a jaded follower in Columbus' footsteps. But like Marlow, Brown cannot resist the inexorable tug of this seediness – almost a Zolaesque 'nostalgie de la boue'. As Brown confesses, in an admission reminiscent of *Journey without Maps* . . . 'I felt a greater tie here, in the shabby land of terror, chosen for me by chance.'[14]

It is through Brown's gloomy, brooding consciousness that the events of the story are filtered. His withering gaze zeroes in on human frailty and feeds on man's weakness. Greene's world becomes gloomily predictable in the eyes of the jaded narrator. David Lodge complains about 'the permeation of his later work with negative and sceptical attitudes, characteristically filtered through the consciousness of a laconic, disillusioned narrator'.[15] Brown is the typically world-weary, lucidly disabused narrator of Greene's stories. He stands in obvious contrast to the naive Smiths. As he admits . . . 'transcience was my pigmentation' . . . and this cosmopolitan, middle-aged 'viveur' makes it impossible for Greene's Haitian novel to be politically engagé. Sartre, not unexpectedly, realized the reactionary nature of this choice of narrative viewpoint. In remarking on the same narrative ploy in Maupassant's stories, Sartre describes this type of narrator as

> . . . an older man, who has seen a lot, read a lot and learnt a lot. . . . He has reached that point in life when . . . man is free from passions and considers those he has experienced with lucid indulgence.[16]

With all passion spent, this narrator is incapable of new enthusiasms. In any case his sense of the ironic vicissitudes of life is too intense for him to be optimistic about the future. The moral and political squalor of Haiti allows Brown to make mordant observations on infidelity, death and human frailty. Haiti's 'Otherness' only confirms Brown's belief that it is just another Conradian 'blank space' where man has sunk back to a primeval state.

In the 1960s *The Comedians* became a model of textual intelligibility. In the same way that the Congo was made intelligible or 'vraisemblable' by Conrad, Greene's master text made Haiti familiar and disturbingly memorable in 1966. *The Comedians* provides an important example of the capacity of the text to produce an imaginative discourse that would make the subject it treats visible in a particular way. As Said explains, in a different context, . . .

> Expertise is attributed to it. The authority of academics, institutions, and governments can accrue to it, surrounding it with still greater prestige than its practical successes warrant. Most important, such texts can *create* not only knowledge but also the very reality they appear to describe.[17]

What gave Greene's text even greater authority was that it fitted into a particular tradition of writing about Haiti. This tradition or discourse had a level of credibility that no well-intentioned anthropology could dispel. Haiti's 'otherness' was as memorable as it was ineradicable. Given the bizarre credibility of the world of *The Comedians*, few would be interested in the social and political reality of Duvalier's regime. Who really were the Tonton Macoutes? How did Duvalier really manage to maintain control? Why were the majority of Haitians so submissive? These were only some of the questions that found misleading answers in Greene's fiction. The 'signs' in the text were so seductive that they eclipsed the 'referent'. *The Comedians* would be credited with an expertise that *Heart of Darkness* once enjoyed. It would in turn establish a discourse that would make similar writing on Haiti both possible and desirable.

Greene's fictional testimony could not have come at a more opportune moment in relations between Haiti and the United States. Relations between the two states had deteriorated rapidly since 1963 when the Kennedy administration openly condemned the Duvalier government. Because of the intensifying crisis, American citizens were advised to leave Haiti. Tales of horror were spread by the evacuees. Duvalier in turn, responded defiantly by asking for the removal of the United States Naval and Air Force mission – led by Marine Colonel Robert Heinl, who would write his own lurid testimony. The United States recalled its Ambassador and diplomatic relations were suspended. Relations improved only after the death of President Kennedy and an uneasy calm prevailed in the following years. The new timorous American Ambassador – Benson Timmons III – signified the reluctant accommodation of Duvalier's regime by an American administration, which was more concerned with the spread of Castro's influence in the region than with Duvalier's human rights record. Schuyler Wilson at the end of *The Comedians* is meant to represent this cynical tolerance of Duvalier in the name of anti-communism. The political marginalization of Haiti from the mid-1960s reinforced the persuasiveness of Greene's stereotypes in the Western imagination. One should not minimize the brutality of the Duvalier regime. But it is surely unwarranted to see Haitian politics as black lunacy. Yet this was the abiding impression left by Greene's account of Haiti as the throbbing organic centre of darkness in the Western Hemisphere.

Even when imaginative literature, written in this period, did not focus on contemporary Haitian politics, it construed the historical past in terms of wildly sensationalist images. For instance, Benjamin Levin's novel *Black Triumvirate* (1972) reveals the extent to which the central figures of Haitian Independence had now become part of a trail of blood and violence that led inexorably to Duvalierism. In a novel that favours the use of the exclamation mark, Levin recounts Haitian history as one frenzied sexual or political encounter after another. His historical voyeurism produces a text bristling with conical breasts, swollen nipples and frenetic thrusts. Such a novel of frenzied convulsions, had an obvious readership in the 1970s. As the blurb correctly states, it is a 'story of sun-drenched sensuality . . . and hair raising violence'. Levin's forgettable novel is merely an index of the imaginative stereotypes that determined Haiti's visibility during the Duvalier regime. Greene had simply provided this discourse with a greater authority and conviction in *The Comedians*. Unfortunately, this tradition of writing was not exclusive to fiction. Historical and political accounts of Haiti and Duvalierism borrowed heavily from Greene's imaginative discourse.

'The horror! The horror!' the final exclamation of dying Kurtz echoes through political accounts of Haiti in the 1960s and 1970s. These works invariably set out to prove to a scandalized audience the extent to which Haiti had slipped away from the values of the civilized world. Such was the conclusion of the widely read *Papa Doc: the Truth about Haiti Today* which was published in 1969. The authors Bernard Diederich and Al Burt saw Duvalier's regime – 'the horror of the hemisphere' and 'the bloodiest tyranny in the hemisphere' – as an obstacle that prevented Haiti from making 'its way into the twentieth century'. The writers authenticated the truth of Greene's novel[18] and Greene obligingly wrote the introduction to their book. In his introduction, Greene correctly sums up the image of Haiti offered by Diederich and Burt as 'tragic, terrifying, bizarre, even at times comic'. The authors claim that their narrative is frank and non-sensationalist but the book is advertised as an account of 'Atrocities in the Realm of a Madman' and of the 'Devil in Paradise'. The image of Duvalier sitting 'in his bath wearing his top hat for meditating: the head of his enemy Philogenes stands on his desk', is dismayingly repeated in the book.

The mixture of fact and fiction in *Papa Doc* is almost inextricable. Footnoted evidence is as calmly reported as scandalous hearsay. With a novelist's precision, the authors include details that are either deflating or comical, such as a Communist writer's nasal voice; Duvalier's drooping eyelids; a houngan's diarrhoea in the National Palace; an enemy's head in an ice bucket. Along with these graphic details goes a disconcerting omniscience on the part of the authors. We have eye-witness accounts of a shoot-out in Kenscoff; a vivid testimony of the stoning of the writer Alexis and even a domestic quarrel in the National Palace during which Madame Duvalier is beaten and pudgy Jean-Claude locks his father in an adjoining room. We are left with the impression of a nightmarish world in which all is possible. The inevitable chapter on Voodoo is included and we are told that orgasms are not infrequent at these ceremonies. Haiti is a land possessed or 'mounted' by a diabolical force. Duvalier's actions are explained as symptoms of mental disorder – paranoia and megalomania.

> ... personality conflicts of a small, physically frail doctor who dreamed of being Dessalines ... he became in his mind a messiah called to lead his people, his children, to reward and punish them as necessary.[19]

The authority and credibility of Diederich and Burt's book on ten years of Duvalier's rule derives as much from their actual knowledge of certain incidents as the imaginative accumulation of unsavoury details.

Another similar personal testimony is Robert Heinl's *Written in Blood* (1978). Heinl, a Marine Colonel, arrived in Haiti in 1959 heading a military mission to train Duvalier's army. In Haitian–

American relations history not only repeats itself but it seems that American Marines repeat each other. Heinl's account of Haiti's 'tragic, ironic and bizarre' history is reminiscent of John Huston Craige's *Cannibal Cousins* (1934) written during the American Occupation. From Dessalines to Duvalier, Heinl develops his vision of Haiti's bloody regression into darkness. He, not unpredictably, justifies the American Occupation since the United States could no longer 'tolerate Haiti's mounting instability' and the 'utter disintegration, in a place and time where perceived American interests' were at stake. The link with Craige is uncanny when it comes to his praise for the 'popularity' of the 'corvée' camps[20] which inexplicably led to a short-lived peasant revolt against the Marines. He like Craige dismisses James Weldon Johnson as an opportunist because of the latter's reports of Marine atrocities. Like his Marine predecessor he felt it was the duty of the United States to put an end to the tragic lunacy of Haitian history.

As is to be expected, Heinl cites approvingly Greene as well as Deiderich and Burt. Greene is now keeping strange company because Heinl is fiercely anti-Communist. Greene criticized the anti-Communist paranoia of the United States and the consequent support for brutal rightist regimes. Heinl combines Green's nightmarish imagery with his own political simplifications. In his view, Jacques Roumain is a rabid Communist. Hughes, Depestre, Alexis and Brierre (!) are all part of a Communist conspiracy.[21] *Written in Blood* is at its lurid best on the Duvalier regime. He talks about seances to capture Kennedy's soul and former Nazis as secret advisers to the government. Unrestrained and unoriginal, Heinl's book demonstrates how durable the images of Haitian barbarism are in the American imagination.

This deep belief in the deviant nature of Haitian society would extend beyond the personal testimonies of Greene, Heinl and Diederich to influence supposedly disinterested and scientific examinations of Haiti. Robert Rotberg's *Haiti: the Politics of Squalor* (1971) provides a view of Haitian society typical of the accounts of the late 1960s and early 1970s. Haiti was once more reduced to a bizarre spectacle of 'overlapping, highly diverse, often contradictory and sometimes startling images'. The metaphor of disease prevails throughout the text. For instance, in discussing the American Occupation, Rotberg sees Haiti as 'a sick society' whose 'fundamental structural malaise' the United States did not cure. Retaining the images of a terminally diseased society, Rotberg gloomily confesses that

> American diagnoses were superficial and did not immediately contribute to a cure for the disease . . . no simple surgery or symptomatic drug was sufficient.[22]

Rotberg quotes Col. Heinl in support of the view that the blood was being drained from this unprotesting body by Dr Duvalier with 'a suction pump'.

The pathological nature of Haitian society was explained by Rotberg as the result of the peculiar 'mental configuration of non-elite Haitians'. According to his theory 'child rearing patterns may provide one of the keys to Haitian political problems'. His deterministic hypothesis set out to prove that black Haitians were deficient in 'fundamental ego-sustaining and ego-developing nurturance'. This dependency complex meant that the Haitian masses favoured political autocracy. They were simply not ready for representative government.

> Haitians therefore can be said to need and expect strong dictatorship; accordingly, democratic politics revives the kinds of tensions which Haitians would prefer to avoid and decisions which they find difficult to make.[23]

Judging from his footnotes, Rotberg had not heard of O. Mannoni's *La Psychologie de la Colonisation* (1950) – which was translated as *Prospero and Caliban* in 1956. Mannoni, in analysing Malagasy society, came to the conclusion that their dependence and insecurity in the face of French colonization was due to a deep dependency complex that goes back to childhood. They, like Haitians, desperately needed paternal authority which in the case of Madagascar resulted in chronic dependence on the French. As Aimé Cesaire declared in *Discourse on Colonialism* (1955) . . . 'You know the old refrain: The Negroes-are-big-children.'[24] Rotberg was advancing his version of a theory that has its roots in deep racial prejudice. His was the most depressing account of the Duvalier regime because unlike Greene, Heinl and Diederich he could not imagine Haitians as behaving differently. Given their 'mental configuration' there would always be a 'paranoid and megalomaniac' President like Duvalier to take advantage of them. Emasculated and submissive, they were doomed to remain in their world of darkness.

By the mid-1970s Haiti had become in the American imagination, essentially a 'sign' ensnared in a fixed, closed discourse that had its origins in *Heart of Darkness*. Accounts of Haiti under Duvalier attest to the pervasiveness and hypnotic power of Conrad's fictional discourse. Greene's *The Comedians*, with its imaginative structure so firmly rooted in Conrad's world, had an important role to play in the process of the textualizing of Haiti at this time. It should also be noted that it was not simply a question of symbolic values and literary representation but that Greene's enabling fiction was part of a particular tradition in writing. Greene's essentially anti-modernist narrative was modelled on such non-fictional forms as the travelogue, the eye-witness account, the diary. It ultimately belongs to that tradition in novel writing that seeks to interpret, to establish order, to reveal the binary system that can organize raw experience. The more disturbing the experience, the greater the need for the organizing power of such fictions. *The Comedians* was the needed fictional response to Haiti under Duvalier and Greene's novel produced other texts that were really testimonial narratives – attempting to combine an authenticating historical discourse with their extravagant contexts. A reversal of such a discourse that made Haiti sinisterly visible would be possible only in a work that departed conceptually from this narrative tradition – one that questioned the smug certainties of interpretation. Such a postmodernist work was Ishmael Reed's black comedy *Mumbo Jumbo* (1972) which seeks to retrieve Haiti from stereotypes, persuasively established in the pretexts of Greene and Conrad.

Reed's text rejects any attempt to interpret as essentially illusory or falsely reassuring – or perhaps a means of rationalizing cultural and political hegemony. The plot turns on the comic deflating of a Conradian discourse as it is white America that is on the defensive because of an epidemic spread of blackness. The hilarious potential of Marlow's horror because of a remote kinship with the primeval bush generates the comic reversals of the novel. Reed is interested not in conventional imagery or self-aggrandizing discourse but in the uncertainties and wild possibilities that human experience can generate. As Henry Louis Gates concludes

... Reed posits the notion of aesthetic play: the play of the tradition, the play on the tradition, the sheer play of indeterminacy itself.[25]

In order to achieve this goal of 'indeterminacy', *Mumbo Jumbo* functions as a parody of the conventions of detective fiction. To the 'truth' of Haiti's 'Otherness' that was advanced in the fiction of Greene and his literary progeny, Reed's demythifying text suggests the impossibility of establishing any truth whatsoever. 'Jes grew' that ineradicable symposium of black culture is incapable of representation. 'Jes grew' is a disease of transgression. It subverts all that is systematic, restrained and cerebral. In contrast to some plagues which 'caused the body to waste away, Jes Grew enlivened the host'. 'Jes Grew', the anti-plague, is a pun on 'Jest' – a subversive humour – and its source is Haiti.

The American Occupation is explained as just another effort on the part of the repressed 'Wallflower Order' to exterminate the cause of 'Jes Grew'. The Haitian occupation of the United States has begun.

More books concerning Haiti have been checked out of American libraries in a week than in the previous history of the library system. To add to that, people walk all over New York speaking Creole and wearing tropical clothes . . .[26]

In order to prevent the further contamination of the United States, war is declared on Haiti.

The Wallflower Order launched the war against Haiti in hopes of allaying Jes Grew symptoms by attacking their miasmatic source. But little Haiti resists. It becomes a world-wide symbol for religious and aesthetic freedom. When an artist happens upon a new form he shouts 'I have Reached My Haiti!'[27]

In a comic reversal of Conrad's discourse, it is the African explorer who appears grotesque. The wooden figure of a Portuguese explorer, carved in a monkey-like posture and seated on a barrel, is taken from Africa by those who 'did not realize that the joke was on them'. Those who were once the object of representation are shown to have the capacity to strike back with humour. This explains why, when this infectious laughter begins to take possession of American citizens, . . . 'Holy Wars have been launched against Haiti under the cover of bringing stability to the Caribbean.' Repression of Haiti is part of the global struggle against Dionysos.

A recognizably un-American account is given of the Occupation by the houngan Benoit Battraville – who along with Charlemagne Péralte actually led the peasant uprising against the Marines. The Occupation is explained as having deeper motives than economic exploitation. It was a war launched by the militant Wallflower Order in their historic struggle against 'Jes Grew'. The 'corvée' law which was introduced to supply forced labour for road-building was just another example of the humourlessly utilitarian nature of the American Occupation. The betrayal and murder of Charlemagne Péralte as well as the role of James Weldon Johnson and the NAACP form part of this view of the Occupation. As a central part of this comic fantasy, Haiti determines to some extent the characters who play important roles in Reed's novel. For instance, Biff Musclewhite is a caricature of the hard-boiled Marine Major – 'the man who tamed the wilderness'. He is the curator of 'the New York Center of Art Detention' and part of the aggressive activity of the Wallflower Order. Opposed to him are Papa LaBas and T. Malice, both of whom are figures from Haitian folk culture who represent the resourcefulness and cunning of the Haitian folk imagination. LaBas is the equivalent of Legba the Voodoo god of the crossroads whose frail, ageing exterior conceals enormous strength. Situated at the frontier of that binary system that separates terrestrial from celestial, he holds the key to the mystery of all signs. In the text he holds the key to 'Jes Grew' – that state of the freed imagination that leads to artistic glossolalia or could find representation only in *Mumbo Jumbo*.

The black humour of Reed's novel is totally different from the Greene's ironic narrative. In Greene's text the humour is at the expense of Haiti in particular and of human naivety in general. Reed's novel is a critique of any discourse that attempts to fix 'signs' in a closed and unchanging way. The diseased body of blackness in Greene's novel is replaced by the rejuvenating force of 'Jes Grew' in Reed. The rhetorical conventions that govern Greene's perception and representation of Haiti are based on a rigid dichotomy that divides Haiti from the rest of the Western world. Reed's *Mumbo Jumbo* is an important exception because, in satirizing the system that underlies this cultural 'dualism', Reed frees Haiti imaginatively from an imposed 'Otherness'.

RE-MEMBERING THE BLACK BODY

> I am possessed by the Other: the Other's look fashions my body in its nakedness, causes it to be born, sculptures it . . .
> J.-P. Sartre, *Being and Nothingness*

Images of obscene visibility, of a deviant physicality have haunted Haiti and Haitians since the early 1960s. The Western imagination reinforced its power over Haiti by objectifying it in a discourse of moral fallenness and corrupt carnality. It is the paranoia implicit in this attitude that Ishmael Reed comically exploits when he describes the symptoms of the Haitian epidemic 'Jes Grew' as physical excess and moral disorientation. Such a discourse can be explained in terms of Michel Foucault's notion of 'dividing practices' which are the means of manipulating and controlling the group upon which a separate identity is conferred. Fallenness and animality are the conditions that necessitate exclusion. As Foucault states in *Madness and Civilisation*

> . . . it was this animality of madness which confinement glorified, at the same time that it sought to avoid the scandal inherent in the immorality of the unreasonable.[28]

Obstracism is the penalty that must be paid for cultural deviance. In December 1972 'Detention Facilities' or 'Processing Centres' were established to deal with the first wave of Haitian refugees washed up on the shores of Florida. This was the sobering experience that awaited thousands of Haitians fleeing economic hardship and political persecution. Jean-Claude Charles is correct when he describes these camps as the 'univers concentrationnaire' which lurks behind 'de si jolies petites plages' in Florida, the Bahamas and Puerto Rico.[29]

The sense of being fixed by the disdainful stare of a scandalized world is the psychological legacy of Duvalierism. The disorienting experience of having to live with, or perhaps in spite of, the distorting stereotypes is part of the poignant testimony of recent Haitian writing. As Jean-Claude Charles admits, the difficulty with understanding Haiti is tied to the received ideas that prevent comprehension

> ... la difficulté pour l'opinion de percevoir la réalite haïtienne au-delà des appareils conceptuels figés ou des observations touristiques, au-delà des chiffres ou des codes narratifs glacés.[30]
>
> (... the difficulty for (world) opinion to perceive the truth about Haiti beyond the fixed conceptual apparatus or the tourists' perspective, beyond the statistics or the frozen descriptive codes.)

To a large extent this distorting discourse uses images of the body or a biological base in order to establish Haiti's 'Otherness'. The black body is bound up with a system of subjugation and relations of power. It is the terrible reality of inhabiting flesh that is shunned as fallen or corrupt that haunts Haitian attitudes to the United States. In language reminiscent of Frantz Fanon's *Black Skin, White Masks*, Charles reflects on the impossibility of establishing individual authenticity in the face of

> ... le regard qui crée la figure majuscule du nègre en laquelle se réduit chaque nègre chacune de mes formes de vie se transforme en un mythe je ne sens plus mes mains mes jambes deviennent flasques mes paupières s'alourdissent tableau clinique d'un cas de possession oui par l'oeil du maître.[31]
>
> (... the look that fashions the collective image of the black man in which each black individual is absorbed each aspect of life is transformed into a myth I can no longer feel my hands my legs become weak my eyelids grow heavy ... a clinical representation of a case of possession yes by the master's look)

This mythifying look was at its most intense in the United States. The feeling of rootlessness and ceaseless wandering is further heightened by the fact that this body has already been humiliated by the black dictatorship of François Duvalier. Consequently, exile becomes the essential experience of the world for the new diaspora of Haitian 'nègres errants' or 'voyageurs sans mots'.

The brutal suppression of all potential centres for political opposition is a feature of Duvalier's regime in the early 1960s. The subsequent exodus of Haitian intellectuals and writers is the subject of Jean Jonassaint's aptly entitled work *Le pouvoir des mots, les maux du pouvoir* (1986) – The Power of Works, the Evils of Power. Since 1961, the date which marks the murder of Jacques Stephen Alexis by Duvalier's troops, . . . 'several Haitian writers have taken the risk of living in exile, but also living their exile'.[32] Jonassiant's study of recent writing in exile is made up of a series of interviews and extracts from various novels and inevitably touches the issue of the ambiguity of exile. Most of these writers faced political persecution in Haiti and cannot afford to be blindly nostalgic about the world they left behind. They now find themselves in situations where they have access to a vast number of books and publication facilities, even if they are uneasy in their new environments. Jonassiant speculates that the trend is towards not only an exploration of the issues of

> . . . wandering, uprooting, exile, migration but also to integrate all languages, all cultures from these diverse places where migrations led.[32]

The modern Haitian writer is very much a refugee driven across borders and cultures, who must now come to terms with his exile and the reality of living in the United States which supported the regime which persecuted him.

As political repression increased and economic hardships intensified, Haitians of all sectors of the society began to come to terms with the economic and political reality of the United States. The distrust and suspicion of earlier years gave way to a painful realization among many that the United States could mean physical and economic survival. Those who chose to stay in Haiti were very vocal about America's racism and imperialism. It indirectly explained their refusal to leave and condemned those who did so. The crusty and staunchly nationalistic Emile Roumer, in his collection of poems *Le caiman étoilé* (The Star Spangled Alligator) (1936), is fiercely critical of American designs on the Caribbean.

> L'indigène est en proie aux monsters en Kaki quand s'élève, la nuit, au cauchemar des îles l'affreux glapissement du caïman yanki![33]
>
> (The native is the prey of the monsters in khaki when there rises, in the night, like an island nightmare the horrible bark of the Yankee alligator!)

For Roumer 'American' rhymes with 'coquin' and 'requin' and these satirical verses remain firmly anchored in the tradition of indigenous militancy of the 1920s. They are recognized only as products of the early 1960s because of the celebratory references to Fidel Castro and the Cuban Revolution. However, Roumer's undaunted faith in the capacity of Haiti to survive, in a humane fashion, the Duvalier regime is shared by few. Curiously, while Roumer is alert to Yankee machinations in the Caribbean, he is silent on the subject of Duvalier's reign of terror in Haiti.

Given the paranoid nature of the Duvalier regime, literary activity in Haiti decreases dramatically. Major writers from Haiti are in Dakar, Paris, Montreal and New York. The question or the reality of leaving Haiti is an important consideration among those who remain within Haiti. The temptation to migrate – particularly to the United States – and fear of exile are themes in one of Haiti's most important writers, who has never left Haiti. Franck Etienne's *Mûr à crever* (1968) – *Ripe for bursting* – is situated in a lower middle-class urban setting where migration is a major preoccupation. Conversations concern those who marry American citizens in order to get visas. The humiliation of living in hiding before being caught and returned to Haiti. Nevertheless, the United States is seen as the only answer to current difficulties whether it means vocational training or dish washing when you get there.

> L'important c'est d'avoir un pied là-bas. Ça procure des avantages, il nous ouvrira ainsi la route des grandes cités industrielles. Sous peu, toute la famille se fixera à New York. Je ne demande pas mieux. Ici, la vie est devenue im-poss-ible.[34]

> (The important thing is to have one foot over there. That brings advantages, it will open the way to the great industrial cities. In a little while, the whole family will get to New York. That is all I want. Here, life has become im-poss-sible.)

'Là-bas' no longer means Africa but the anticipated comforts of New York, Brooklyn and Miami. Etienne is less shrill in his disapproval than Roumer but they both view migration as a kind of opportunism. In a later play, *Pèlin Tèt* (1978), set in New York, two Haitian migrants, a worker and an intellectual, discuss their experiences. One of them, Piram, finally confesses that his life is so hard in exile that there are no pleasures left for him.

> Aucuns plaisirs; femmes, pas! Cinéma, pas! Alcool, pas! Cigarettes . . . seulement quand tu m'en donnes une . . . je me détruis dans les usines d'ici. Je suis completement epuisé, écrémé, délabré.³⁵

> (No pleasures; no women! No cimena! No alcohol! Cigarettes . . . only when you give me one . . . I am destroying myself in the factories over here. I am completely exhausted, wasted, mashed up.)

Etienne's sobering vision presents the United States not as the 'Promised Land' but as hell itself. The intellectual shows the worker the self-delusion that blinds the latter to the grim reality of New York.

This is also the general idea in *Le Chant des Sirènes* (1979) by Marie Thérèse Colimon. As the title implies, Haitians have fallen victim – like Homer's sailors – to the enchanted voices of those who will lure them to destruction. These short stories, a little old-fashioned like the title, present one case study after another of the damage caused to human relationships because of the need to succeed in the United States. From the outset the hardships of exile are described – the fear of being attacked, the frenzied pace, the long hours and the distrust of the new environment. Yet the motivation to leave is always implicit in the tiny, shabby, overcrowded rooms of Port-au-Prince where hunger is ever present. As in Franck Etienne's novel, there is a pathological obsession with 'Là-bas'. One has the impression of an entire nation 'in transit', of a people waiting for exit visas. All activity is concentrated on the airport lobby before the arrival of the flight from Miami.

> Il y en avait qui partaient tout simplement. Il y en avait qui s'envolaient. Il y en avait qui s'enfuyaient. Il y en avait qui fuyaient. Celui-ci, le chomâge et la misère; celui-là, les échecs et les deceptions.³⁶

> (There were those who were simply departing. There were those who were flying away. There were those who were running away. There were those who were escaping. This one, unemployment and misery; that one, failures and disappointment.)

The dream of the 'good life' in the United States is uninterrupted. Like the characters in a Maupassant short story, they live in a world of illusion, all waiting for their turn to go off to 'ce beau Paradis sur terre!' (this beautiful earthly Paradise). In one story a child fantasizes about the life of his parents who have taken a boat for the 'pays l'aut'bô' (the land over there). He imagines a world of food, gadgets and colour television. The reality lived by his parents is sadly different from his dreams. His father is a waiter and his mother a domestic. The misguided child is symbolic of those who spend their entire lives waiting for deliverance in the 'pays l'aut'bô'. All roads lead there. The countryside is deserted; the capital just a temporary stop on the way to the airport.

One recurring motif in Colimon's stories is the desertion of the mother by her children, who ultimately abandon her. Colimon is as critical of the conditions that force Haitians to migrate – even though she carefully steers clear of politics – as the tendency to deny the past after living in the United States. Perhaps one of the most moving stories concerns an old woman, deserted by her children, who dies alone. She is left with only memories and some photographs. Her life is one of an endless debilitating wait.

> Peu-à-peu, elle était devenue cette chétive chose recroquevillée et solitaire qui ne vivait plus que dans l'attente du passage du facteur.[37]
>
> (Little by little, she had become that sickly creature, wizened and alone, only living in the hope that the postman would pass by.)

The story concentrates not on the mother's tragic decline but on the funeral when she dies. Colimon's most caustic satire is reserved for those who, filled with remorse, rush back to Haiti. The funeral is described as a 'sinister comedy' and Colimon has a devastatingly sharp eye for the deflating detail which reveals the ludicrousness of those who return. She focuses on the fraudulent grief and the general histrionics of the funeral, the blonde wife and the 'Pan-Am' travelling bag that are symbols of success. The narrator leaves the funeral to return to her own child and the same process is about to be repeated. She will become in turn just another 'dans la longue chaîne de mères . . . comme la disparue si regrettée maintenant . . .' (in long chain of mothers . . . like the deceased so sadly missed now). The irony and the fatalism of the end point to the levels of dislocation felt within Haiti because of the mythification of the United States as the land of supermarkets and colour television. It is the consequent disruption of human relationships and the distortion of values that concern writers who remain in Haiti. For obvious reasons, the case of the political exile is not treated in work published in Haiti. They cling to a nationalistic defence of Haiti as the 'Mère-Patrie' deserted for the materialistic temptations of the United States.

The nostalgia and guilt that are inevitably part of the experience of exile can be seen in Emile Ollivier's novel *Mère-Solitude* (1983) which can be seen as a response to Colimon's stories of the abandoned mother. As Ollivier himself says, the main character's search for the secret of his mother's death is an allegory of the larger quest for identity, cultural as well as personal. His name Narcès suggests the self-scrutiny of the mythological Narcissus and his journey reveals that nothing has changed in Haiti since the colonial period. The repeated cycle of human destructiveness and waste is constantly repeated.[38] The Haitian self-image is by the mid-1970s marked by the humiliations and the violence inflicted by Duvalierism. A literary discourse emerges, which is built around the image of the defiled body. Etienne in his novel *Dézafi* (1975) focuses on the zombified body inarticulate and submissive. It is subject to spasms and convulsions as it represses the violence that should be the natural reaction to its condition of intense and excessive pain.

> Avoir la langue engourdie ou cisaillée en mille morceaux. Etre repu. Avoir les tripes encordées par la douleur. Eprouver une soif d'enfer. . . . S'enliser dans la mort. Mais qui parmi nous vit réellement? Vraiment, qui?
> Une infinité de gens, les plus divers, sombrent en pleine conscience dans un rève hallucinant.[39]

> (To have one's tongue grow numb or sliced into a thousand pieces. To be full. To have our guts twisted with grief. To feel a thirst for hell . . . To slide down to death. But who among us really lives? Really, who?
> Countless people, all different kinds, sink fully conscious into a hallucination.)

In Etienne's novel Haiti is symbolized by the cramped and viscous world of Bois-Neuf, in which a malevolent 'houngan' Sintil rules over the unprotesting passivity of his zombified community. Exile is no longer a condition exclusive to those who went away. Within Sintil's sinister world one was also forced to experience a paralyzing alienation and an interminable wandering. Behind Sintil there can be discerned the shadowy presence of American interests – the railways of the Mac-Donald Company and the sisal fields of SHADA.

In *Dézafi* Etienne conceives of contemporary politics as a constant and degrading gravitational pull that drags everyone into a world of flaccid flesh and pervasive slime. The imaginative universe of literature written by Haitians in exile is necessarily different. Theirs is a world of ceaseless change and movement, as anonymously open as Sintil's is oppressively closed. Etienne's living dead dream of being; the exile undergoes continuous metamorphosis. The complications of exile and the open-ended nature of this condition are described by René Depestre who has been more or less in exile since 1946. He points to the several levels on which exile can exist. To him growth implies the creation of several 'moi successifs'. As he has had to leave behind religious, ideological and moral restraint, so exile emerges as the natural mental state of the poet who must establish his credentials because of self-transcendence and imaginative daring. He recently expressed the need to redefine the notion of exile.

> Il me faut dépasser la vision de l'exil que notre temps partage encore avec l'antiquité, la renaissance, l'âge romantique. A ces trois époques, en effet, la notion d'exil évoque un être qui arraché à son pays natal, . . . subit sur une terre étrangère une douloureuse expérience de nostalgie et de deuil.[40]
>
> (I have to transcend the vision of exile that our age still shares with antiquity, the Renaissance, the Romantic era. At these three periods, in fact, the notion of exile evokes someone who torn from his native land . . . undergoes on foreign soil a painful experience of nostalgia and grief.)

Depestre defines exile as an almost inevitable process of ceaseless transformation. He had from the 1950s challenged the idea of identity as fixed and static when he rejected Senghor's (and Duvalier's) notion of negritude as romantic and reactionary mystification. In his writing, the poetic self is not an objectified subject but a creature capable of ceaseless self-renewal. In Depestre's poetry spiritual liberation is the imaginative equivalent of carnal triumph.

The corporeal imagery of Depestre's poetry written in exile can be defined by what Bakhtin termed 'a grotesque realism'. In contrast to the world of the finished and complete . . . 'The grotesque image reflects a phenomenon in transformation, an as yet unfinished metamorphosis, of death and birth, growth and becoming'.[41] This dream of carnal renewal becomes increasingly explicit in his poetry written during the 1960s. For instance, he celebrates in his *Journal d'un animal marin* (1964) a vision of the unrestrained, reanimated body.

> Je chante . . . nos corps nus émerveillés,
> nos membres éblouis![42]
>
> (I celebrate . . . our wonder-struck bodies,
> our dazzled limbs!)

A poetic realization of euphoric sensuality transcends all dichotomy, subverts a fixed, divisive discourse. The defiled body is imaginatively reconstructed in Depestre's exemplary eroticism. In the long poem *Un arc-en-ciel pour l'occident chrétien* (1967) this militant sexuality is deployed against the morbidly puritanical United States.

In this work described as 'poème-mystère vaudou' Depestre situates his sexual subversion of a repressed white world in the context of a Voodoo ceremony. It is a grand vision of human regeneration as the poet, possessed by his gods, offers what Bakhtin called 'a bodily and popular corrective to individual idealistic and spiritual pretence'. Depestre is interested in Voodoo not as an African retention but as an example of 'surréalisme populaire' – an earthly assault on high-minded and fraudulent establishment values.

> Il y a dans le vodou cette association du mysticisme et de l'érotisme: un dieu phallique, Legba, est le dieu principal du

vodou. . . . C'est une religion éminemment érotique, un érotisme naturel . . .⁴³

(There is in Voodoo this association of mysticism and eroticism: a phallic god, Legba, is the main god of Voodoo. . . . It is an eminently erotic religion, a natural eroticism . . .)

Within the dramatic rituals of Voodoo, Depestre finds a vehicle for a hedonistic self-affirmation. Depestre's revolution is a carnal and erotic one as all hierarchies collapse and contradictions dissolve before the onslaught of the poet's virility!

The early section of *Un arc-en-ciel pour l'occident chrétien* concentrates on the process of self-definition as the body possessed becomes increasingly powerful and aggressive.

> Oui je suis un nègre-tempête
> Un nègre racine – d'arc-un-ciel
> Mon coeur se serre comme un poing.⁴⁴

> (Yes I am a black man-storm
> A rooted-rainbow black man
> My heart is clenched like a fist.)

There follows a litany of self-definition as the body breaks free from a restrictive biology ('Je fais exploser ma biologie') and asserts a Protean capacity for infinite transformations. A new spiritually and physically mobilized self is set free

> Me voici un nègre tout neuf
> Je me sens enfin moi-même
> Dans ma nouvelle géographie solaire.⁴⁵

> (Here I am a brand new black man
> I feel myself at last
> In my new solar geography).

He directs this new physical and sexual energy (le volcan de ma nègrerie) against a repressed and repressive 'Christian West'.

In Depestre's sexual fantasy, his virile 'alter ego' humiliates the quintessential white American family. Depestre imagines the 'all American' family of a judge in Alabama as the heartless and puritanical centre of culture bent on militarism and destruction.

Une famille bien américaine
Participant à fond à tout ce qui
Mene l'Amérique à la catastrophe[46]

(An all American family
Profoundly a part of all that which
leads America to catastrophe.)

The white males are all either soldiers, senators or future ambassadors – part of a sinister political apparatus. It is an easy progression from the sexual repression of the Alabama family to the 'American gods of the nuclear age' at Omaha. In this picture of capitalist repression, the judge's womenfolk are the ones who are the least guilty. They are themselves victimized by the inhibited sexuality of the Judge's world. They are the ones that the poet sets out to save through his newly discovered pagan sexuality. The time has come for sexual liberation – 'le moment d'arranger/le ventre de chaque femelle de la maison'. He will become a mocking and liberating incarnation of sexual aggression as he rampages through the 'Christian West'. His fiery impersonations are all calculated. The gods that possess him allow for sexual metamorphosis – Legba, Damballah, Chango and the guédé. In the image of the rainbow Depestre attempts to reconcile sexual hubris with spiritual renewal. Liberated imagination, liberated love, liberated body are all incorporated in the engorged, phallic rainbow ('Sexe bandé de l'eau') which is also a symbol of peace and fusion. In his heroic vision of the remembered body Depestre, at least temporarily, escapes from the humiliations of the abject and mutilated flesh that haunts the imagination of other Haitian writers. His Rabelaisian self-exposure is one answer to the exile's imaginative dilemma. For others, a calculated anonymity and a willed self-effacement are the appropriate response to the fixing look of the Western world.[47]

For another Haitian writer in exile, Jean-Claude Charles, rewriting the body does not lead to verbal carnality but to a disincarnate and ascetic vision. For Depestre, the arena of the 'hounfor' (Voodoo temple) is a primordial space within which Depestre seeks sexual confrontation. Charles cannot suspend the haunting reality of the defiled body. He seeks a solution in a space beyond carnality, beyond words. Depestre's exile is as verbose and outspoken as Charles' is hermetic and guarded. Exile, consequently, becomes a strategy for dealing with the stereotype of the 'corps noir'.

> Contrairement à beaucoup d'autres, je considère l'exil comme une chance: la situation d'exil peut parfaitement être une situation productrice . . . je souhaite qu'il se maintienne. Et j'espère bien rester exilé jusqu'au bout.[48]

> (Contrary to many others, I consider exile as an opportunity: the condition of exile can perfectly well be a productive one . . . I want it to be maintained. And I hope to remain an exile to the end.)

Therefore, there is a cultivated elusiveness in Charles' work. Several voices, registers, genres – his 'écriture polygraphique' – are thrown together to create the impression of sustained anonymity. His identity is defined, or not defined, by the incompleteness, fragmentation, evasiveness characteristic of this narrative voice. This undermining of the stable and fixed narrative viewpoint is as much a response to Modernist aesthetics as a manoeuvre to escape the defiled 'corps noir'.

The subject entrapped in 'Otherness' is the theme of *Le corps noir*. The pervasive and defining pressure of the look of the white world as well as the black one.

> Or maîtres d'hier et d'aujourd'hui investissent mon corps, veulent que ça leur produise une plus-value juteuse et me disent la même chose. Les maîtres blancs me disent: Nous avons plein pouvoir sur ton corps; nous sommes son auteur, nous l'écrivons, le décrivons, le déployons, le retournons; nous sommes les pourvoyeurs de sa narration: nous lui donnons son âme. Les maîtres noirs me disent: Nous partageons le même corps; nous sommes le Même dans notre difference; nous partageons la meme âme; nous sommes le Même dans notre identité. . . . Tous définissent mon corps noir, à la mesure des defauts ou des vertus de mon âme noir, appauvrie ou enrichie ou fil de l'hérédité, depuis la malédiction du fils nègre de Noé: Cham.[49]

> (Now masters of yesterday and today take control of my body, want it to produce for them a juicy profit and tell me the same thing. White masters tell me: We have total power over your

body; we are its creator, we write it, describe it, display it, turn it around; we provide its discourse; we give it its soul. Black masters tell me: We share the same body; we are the same in our own way; we share the same soul; we are the same in our identity. . . . They all define black body, in terms of the faults and virtues of my black soul, impoverished or enriched according to my heredity, since the curse of Noah's black son: Ham.)

The witty and sad eccentricities of *Le corps noir* presents a survey of cultural miscellany, from radio broadcasts to history books, in which the defining discourse of the Other is ubiquitous and inescapable. Time has changed nothing and Haiti is that privileged space where the black body is at its most abject and defiled.

. . . 1915 retour du colon lequel ne s'était jamais vraiment absenté cette fois il parle américain do you see my big stick you see it ok. You better believe it monsieur s'installe monsieur fait comme chez lui monsieur est en effet chez lui . . .[50]

(. . . 1915 return of the coloniser who had never really left this time he speaks American do you see my big stick you see it ok. You better believe it the gentleman takes up residence the gentleman makes himself at home the gentleman is really at home . . .)

Charles cannot imagine the ecstatic and potent reincarnation of Depestre. In the place of Depestre's joyful 'géolibertinage' we see Charles' wandering in a world of consoling darkness. He celebrates the fact that his condition of absolute exile provides an escape because it diminishes his visibility.

. . . négre errant j'avance autrement dit toujours dans le noir mais de ce noir que jaillit pour moi la plus folle espérance . . . s'il faut appartenir à quelque race je suis de la race des voyageurs sans mots . . .[51]

(. . . wandering black I go forward as it were always in the dark but from this dark rushes the wildest hope for me . . . if I must belong to some race I am of the race of wordless travellers . . .)

Three of Charles' other works, *Sainte dérive des cochons* (1977) and *de si jolies petites plages* (1982), and the recent *Manhattan Blues* (1985) are about Haitian exile. This time the locale is the United States.

The earlier work, *Sainte dérive des cochons*, as the title implies is about drifting. It is about living in New York and provides the individual case history that would be explored on a broader scale in *Le corps noir*. New York is presented as the heart of 'babylonamerica' in its inhuman pursuit of an antiseptic future. This destructive town . . .

> reve d'un forwest lunaire sans poussière sans microbe sans nègre avec des poubelles cylindriques sur les trottoirs avec des policiers mauves campés devant les abattoirs-penitenciers . . .[52]

> (dreams of a lunar farwest without dust without flies without blacks with cylindrical dustbins on the pavements with policemen in mauve standing before slaughter-house prisons . . .)

The unease of the 'corps noir' in such a world is the source of physical and psychological torture for the exiled Haitian. American imperialism lives in fear of the unknown, of emptiness, which is the world inhabited by the exile. America's attempts to take possession of Vietnam and Haiti simply increase the insecurity of the Haitian exile. Haiti in 1915, Vietnam in 1971 – they both are part of an aggressive plan to refashion or obliterate the 'corps noir'.

> . . . les bombes sur les enfants de vietnam . . . les marines en 1915 dans le baie de port-au-prince on va leur apprendre la civilisation à ces sauvages on va sauver la peau de notre système . . .[53]

> (. . . bombs on the children of vietnam . . . marines in 1915 in the bay of port-au-prince we will teach these savages civilization we will save the skin of our own system . . .)

Together with aggressive imperialism goes an imaginative discourse that reduces the black man to the realm of the biological. The Haitian people are reduced to caricatures of an exhibitionistic sensuality ('quelle négresse hou la la et puis votre peinture naive hou la la' . . .). Such a world has no place for a black body which neither supplies pleasure nor entertainment. This sinister 'village global' has no place for a black poet and his typewriter, whose task is to keep talking ('il ne faut pas cesser de raconter') to prevent the absolute domination of the Other's discourse.

The fate of the Haitian 'boat people' in the United States is an extreme example of the way official policy is based on a discourse that is rooted in a cultural unconscious. The 'Detention Facilities' set up to house the Haitian migrants are a dramatic reaction to fear of contamination by the unknown and the unspeakable. In one case history after another *de si jolies petites plages* traces the tragic story of official American refusal to respond in a human fashion to the desperation of thousands of black refugees. In a style which is more ironic than strident ('A histoire tragique, écriture ironique') Charles views Americans as naive and credulous and apparently unaware of the barbarism in their midst. They believe that

> . . . cette civilisation est immortelle qu'il n'existe qu'une seule Histoire celle du capitalisme sans commencement ni fin les délices du capitalisme réussi tandis qu'à trente-six trente-sept kilomètres de là à la lisière orientale des Everglades au camp de Krome plusieurs centaines d'Haitiens se demandent à quelle sauce ils seront mangés . . .[54]

> (. . . this civilization is immortal that there exists only one History that of capitalism without beginning or end the pleasures of a successful capitalism while thirty-six thirty-seven kilometres from there on the eastern edge of the Everglades in the Krome camp several hundred Haitians wonder how they will be eaten . . .)

In the American response to the 'boat people', Charles sees the inevitable result of years of stereotyping Haiti as the 'heart of darkness'. The 'univers concentrationnaire' of the Haitian migrant is the material and explicit version of a condition of spiritual confinement that all Haitians are forced to endure.

> L'exil, le permanente mobilité, l'incessante migration – y compris de langue, d'écriture –, au-delà de leur détermination extérieure, douloureuse, me sont un bienfait. De toute facon, la prison du monde, par son essentielle inhumanité, nous fait

payer la faute d'être nés. En l'espace ouvert par l'errance, la peine est simplement plus douce, peut-être.⁵⁵

(Exile, permanent mobility, ceaseless migration – including language, writing –, beyond their painful determination from the outside are an advantage to me. In any case, the prison of the world, because of its essential inhumanity, makes us pay for the fault of being born. In the space opened by wandering, the pain is simply less harsh, perhaps.)

A dismembered body finds expression in a dismembered discourse. Exile because it allows for movement, metamorphosis and invisibility is the longed for state. In such a state the Haitian writer must reinvent himself. Charles' view of the fugitive Haitian exile is quite distinct from Depestre's heroic posture. A Baudelairean 'dandysme' seems to grope for . . .

> the asceticism of the dandy who makes his body, his behaviour, his feelings and passions, his very existence, a work of art.⁵⁶

There is no essential self worth discovering for Charles. Indeed the fixing eyes of both 'maitres blancs et noirs' have deformed the exile's existence because of these stereotypes. The only hope is to constantly reinvent oneself, to become a man of several discourses, identities, and styles to escape the monstrous contours of the black body. Charles' texts are constructed not around rediscovery of being but a continuous process of becoming.

The gross antithesis between pure and impure, whole and flawed, has come to dominate perception in all areas of Haitian–American relations. Charles' worst fears about the tragic potential of this stark cultural dichotomy have been realized in the spread of the AIDS virus. Haitians are once more implicated as the villains of the piece. They, because of their historical association with corporal perversion, are now seen as the source of the infection that threatens the United States. Long after the United States Center for Disease Control had cleared Haitians as a high-risk group, the conviction persists that Haitians are congenitally predisposed to physical perversion. The textualizing of Haiti in terms of deviant 'Otherness' persists. For instance, the invidious speculation of David Black in *The Plague Years* (1986) leads him to theorize that biologically Haitians are more susceptible to AIDS, since hopelessness is 'immunosuppressive' and the 'mad-dog dictatorship' of Duvalier has caused Haitians 'to have suppressed immune systems'.

The polarizations that divide Haitians from Americans by the end of the nineteenth century, exist now in a more extreme and intense way than ever before. For Haitians the years after 1960 are a period of excruciating self-consciousness. The sexual hubris of Depestre and the disincarnate ideal of Jean-Claude Charles are two possible responses to the disfiguring stereotypes of perverse and aberrant darkness that the 'Christian West' has imposed on Haiti since the advent of Duvalierism. The black body has become that 'espace invivable' that one must either transform or escape.

6
Epilogue: Caribbean Overtures

> We stared at each other, blood on my face, tears on hers. It was as if I saw myself. Like in a looking-glass.
>
> Jean Rhys, *Wide Sargasso Sea*

In our survey of Haitian–American relations since the nineteenth century, we have seen the human imagination at its most defensive and at its least generous. Even though all imaginative activity springs from ideological roots, it is also expected to have the capacity to alter and liberate systems of belief and human practice. The imaginative constraints we have examined form an inflexible rhetoric of power or a paralysing self-consciousness that not only distances the Other but sadly, inescapably imprisons the subject as well. Genuine attempts to know objectively or to see clearly become increasingly difficult as textually produced 'Otherness' attains an authority and a credibility that permanently obscures the truth. The texts examined do not merely reflect the history of Haitian–American relations. They are a dynamic part of that history – even at times a determining force within it. It is not the 'timelessness' of great art that concerns us nor the autonomy of the individual imagination. Instead, our reading tends to concentrate on the 'timeliness' of writing that subdues and numbs the imagination by resorting to conventions and stereotypes that are part of a popular discourse. This textual discourse imaginatively fixes geopolitical and historical awareness that becomes the controlling perception in scholarly, historical and anthropological texts. At given periods in Haitian–American relations the particulars might change but the underlying configuration remains unaltered. Individual creativity can ultimately do little against the force of such imaginative constraints.

The Caribbean Sea has allowed relations between Haiti and the United States to be tangibly, visually traced. The first refugees who turned up on the shores of the United States were French families fleeing the violence of the Haitian War of Independence at the end of the eighteenth century. By 1915 the ships that find they way to Port-au-Prince are American warships that land Admiral Caperton and his Marines. The mass exodus of black, impoverished refugees from Duvalier's régime retraces the journey made almost two centuries earlier by white colonizers. Migration, exile and domination are responsible for an unceasing traffic across the sea that joins and separates the first Republics in the New World. Yet emotionally and psychologically, this is a Sargasso Sea in that suspicion and insecurity have established a binary vision that reinforces the difference between both groups. A limited and limiting repertoire of responses has resulted which systematically polarizes and mythifies each culture in the eyes of the other.

The United States reinforces its own identity by marginalizing Haiti or reducing it to the status of an underground self ('Cannibal Cousins'). Haitians cling to an Old World francophile identity in order to face the real fears of American ostracism. The detention camps for the 'boat people' and the belief in the Haitian source of the AIDS virus have only justified Haitian fears in this regard. Yet this historical tragedy had idealistic beginnings. The Haitian revolution owed much to the United States. Eugene Genovese notes that

> Of Count d'Estaing's 3,600 French troops at Savannah in 1779, 545 were blacks. To be sure, they participated primarily as servants and menials. But they had eyes, ears and brains and could judge events for themselves. One of them was Henri [sic] Christophe.[1]

Haitian blood is shed in the struggle for American independence. Yet consistently, the United States has refused to be sensitive to the nature of the Haitian revolution and its ambitions. If this were simply a maroon revolt or a slave uprising, the United States could have lived with it. However, Haitians conceived of their Independence struggle not as an effort to re-establish the African village but to found a modern black state. It was the grandeur of this ambition that made the reality of the first black Republic in the New World intolerable to many in the United States. The achievement and the ambition of Haitian leaders would fire the imaginations of oppressed peoples and radical thinkers on both sides of the Atlantic. Again Genovese points out that Haiti was not conceived as 'an oversized maroon colony in the middle of the Caribbean'. The Haitian revolution . . .

> did not aspire to restore some lost African world or build an isolated Afro-American enclave that, whatever its cultural merit, could have played no autonomous role in world affairs and would have had to become a protectorate of one or another European power. Toussaint, and after his death Dessalines and Henri Christophe tried to forge a modern black state.[2]

This signalled the beginning of new possibilities for the West. The Haitian Revolution would inspire New World blacks just as the French Revolution had been an inspiration to white America. It was this influence that was feared and the United States relaxed only when the counter-revolution led by élite interests within Haiti made the possibility of Haitian success unlikely. The United States since then has tended to favour any regime, black or mulatto, from Boyer to Duvalier which reduced Haiti to an impoverished, peasant community.

The history of Haitian–American relations is filled with missed opportunities and tragic incomprehension.[3] American intentions to reshape, control and dominate Haiti because of the latter's threat to its interests, are sustained by an imaginative grid of stereotypes through which Haiti is filtered into America's consciousness. Images of the rebellious body, the repulsive body, the seductive body and the sick body constitute a consistent discourse that has fixed Haiti in the Western imagination. The 'Haitianizing' of Haiti as unredeemably deviant. This mythification of Haiti acquired a special shrillness during the Duvalier years. In response, Haitians attempt to write themselves into existence, to use the written word to defend themselves against the trauma of lived reality. Having been deformed and ostracized corporally, they retrieve themselves imaginatively. There is therapy for the Haitian psyche in the images of aloof patrician, precocious 'nègre', unencumbered dandy or vengeful Eros.

On 7 February 1986 the Duvalier dynasty fell from power. Haiti and the United States stood poised on the threshold of a new relationship. Earlier the United States had ensured the peaceful succession of Jean-Claude to the presidency. Now the United States provided the Air Force cargo plane that spirited away

Haiti's President for Life, Jean-Claude Duvalier, before angry Haitians could get their hands on him. The feeling prevailed that Duvalier's exile in France had solved Haiti's problems. After recording scenes of looting and revenge, the American media have become more fascinated with the consumer excesses of Michèle Duvalier. Tales of her past indiscretions and present lavish life-style are ready-made for prime-time television. However, soap opera fantasy does not prevail among the impoverished people Duvalier left behind. Indeed, Haitians found, on the morning after their revolution, an interim government made up of a few old Duvalierists led by a paternalistic general. In spite of the daring of the anti-Duvalier movement, the mighty have not fallen and the sad legacy of Duvalierism persists.

The United States, which orchestrated the departure of Jean-Claude Duvalier, gained much good will from the role played at the time. However, blind support for the provisional government by Washington has meant a resurgence of confidence among the military and an equal distrust from the Haitian people. A year ago American flags were waved in the streets. Now anti-American slogans have appeared on the walls of the capital, and for the first time in two decades anti-American demonstrations have been organized.

In August 1986 the Secretary of State, George Schultz, made a short stop in Haiti to show his support for the provisional government. He praised General Namphy for setting Haiti on the right track and pronounced the country democratic, without quite defining what he meant. He also offered $6 million worth of 'non-lethal' aid to a largely unreformed Haitian military. Such enthusiastic support for the army is disturbing in the face of a far greater need for economic aid and the less than satisfactory human rights performance by the army. Duvalier kept the military on a tight rein. Washington's support has caused the spectre of militarism to return once more to Haiti's political culture.

Some of the most striking graffiti that have appeared in Port-au-Prince declare 'Schultz Macoute'. It may conjure up an absurdly comical image but does reflect the real fear of United States complicity with the Duvalierist military. The *America's Watch* report on Haiti concludes that 'United States policy has not helped advance human rights' in Haiti. Washington's failure to signal its disapproval could have dire consequences in the future. This comes at a time when everyday Haitian life has been deeply

Americanized. The mesmeric glow of colour television is visible in Haiti's ruined towns. Voodoo priests wear designer clothes and the shrill presence of the transistor radio is pervasive. The United States continues to be seen as the land of opportunity and it is perhaps not too far-fetched to imagine an anglophone Haiti by the next century.

Yet insensitivity and clumsiness seem to haunt relations between Haiti and the United States. For instance, the extermination of a million pigs in 1983 because of swine fever was a disaster for the Haitian peasant. USAID introduced breeding stock from Iowa to replace the slaughtered animals. However, the black Haitian pig could survive on garbage, whereas his white American replacement needs clean water, special pens and specially prepared food. The majority of peasants could not afford such luxuries for themselves – not to mention the pigs! Again Americans are seen as trying to manipulate the situation.

In the tropical heat intentions and reality can become blurred. There has been much talk of a repudiation of the Duvalier past and the establishment of a new democracy. Yet more than a year has passed since Duvalier fell from power and Haitians have little to celebrate. Like the mountains that rise rugged and naked from the plains, Haiti has made a mighty physical effort to break free from the bonds of Duvalierism but it remains exposed and vulnerable. Haiti, like Caliban's island, is now full of noises – but unfortunately noises of pain and frustration. To these cries of self assertion, the United States apparently prefers the muffled groans of the zombi – the ultimate example of unprotesting servitude. Perhaps given the stark polarizations that have haunted relations between Haiti and the United States, they are destined to live unhappily ever after.

Notes

CHAPTER 1: THROUGH THE EYES OF THE OTHER

1. M. Foucault, *The Order of Things* (New York: Vintage, 1973) p. 47.
2. E. Said, *Orientalism* (New York: Vintage, 1979) p. 93.
3. The use of sexual terminology to define racial differences in the nineteenth century is convincingly demonstrated in Christopher Miller's *Blank Darkness* (University of Chicago Press, 1985) p. 122.
4. Regis Antoine develops the theme of the 'feminization' of the Caribbean by French writers in *Les écrivains français et les antilles* (Paris: Maisonneuve et Larose, 1978) pp. 295–306.
5. Harriet Beecher Stowe, *Uncle Tom's Cabin* (New York: Paul Erikson, 1964) p. 23.
6. Ibid., p. 542.
7. Josiah Priest, *Bible Defence of Slavery* (Glasgow: W. S. Brown, 1851) p. 51.
8. John Whittier, *Anti-Slavery Poems* (New York: Arno Press, 1969) p. 18.
9. Ibid., p. 18.
10. R. Logan, *The Diplomatic Relations of the United States with Haiti* (Chapel Hill: University of North Carolina Press, 1941) p. 152.
11. W. Jordan, *White over Black: American attitudes toward the negro* (New York: Norton and Co., 1977) pp. 380–6.
12. P. J. Straudenraus, *The African Colonization Movement 1816–1875* (New York: Columbia University Press, 1961) p. 2.
13. J. N. Léger, *Haiti: Her History and Her Detractors* (New York: The Neale Publishing Co., 1907) p. 303.
14. R. Logan, op. cit., p. 226.
15. Preface to G. Frederickson, *The Black Image in the White Mind* (New York: Harper & Row, 1971).
16. J. Redpath, *A Guide to Hayti* (Westport: Negro Universities Press, 1970) p. 129.
17. M. Child, *The Freedman's Book* (New York: Arno Press, 1969) p. 18.
18. J. Nelson, *The Negro Character in American Literature* (Lawrence: University of Kansas Press, 1926) p. 23.
19. S. Brown, 'The Negro Character as seen by white authors', *The Journal of Negro Education*, vol. 11, no. 2 (Apr. 1933) p. 184.
20. W. W. Brown, *St. Domingo, Its Revolutions and Its Patriots* (Boston, 1855) p. 82.
21. *Correspondence Relative to the Emigration to Haiti of the Free People of Colour in the United States* (New York: Mahlon Day, 1824).
22. Ibid., p. 16.
23. T. Holly, 'Thoughts on Hayti', *The Anglo-African Magazine*, vol. 1 (1859).
24. W. Farrison, *William Wells Brown: Author and Reformer* (University of Chicago Press, 1969) p. 356.

25. R. Léon, *Propos d'histoire d'Haiti* (Port-au-Prince: Imp. de l'Etat, 1945) p. 212.
26. F. Douglass, *Oration at the World's Fair* (Chicago, Jan. 1893). L. Montague, *Haiti and the United States 1714–1938*, also emphasizes Douglass' sensitivity to the Haitian point of view (p. 157).
27. For a fuller treatment see D. Nicholls, *From Dessalines to Duvalier* (Cambridge University Press, 1979) pp. 137–8.
28. Quoted in L. F. Hoffman 'Les Etats Unis et Les Américains dans les lettres haïtiennes', *Etudes Littéraires*, vol. 13, no. 2 (1980) p. 291.
29. D. Delorme, *Réflexious Diverses sur Haiti* (Paris: F. Dentu, 1873) pp. 126–7.
30. F. Hibbert, *Le manuscrit de mon ami* (Port-au-Prince: Imp. Chéraquit, 1923) p. 98.
31. D. Delorme, op. cit., p. 128.
32. M. Coicou, *Poésies Nationales* (Paris: Imp. Jourdan, 1892) p. 124.
33. T. Guilbaud, 'John Brown' in Saint-Louis and Lubin, *Panorama de la poésie haitienne* (Port-au-Prince: Henri Deschamps, 1950) p. 86.
34. E. Laforest, 'John Brown' in *Sonnets – médaillons du dix-neuvième sièce* (Paris: Librairie Fischbacher, 1909) p. 183.
35. D. Delorme, op. cit., p. 124.
36. Quoted in Rulx Léon, *Propos d'histoire d'Haiti* (Port-au-Prince, 1945) p. 205.
37. E. Balch, *Occupied Haiti* (New York: Negro University Press, 1969) p. 120.
38. F. Marcelin, *Choses Haitiennes* (Paris: Imp. Kugelmann, 1896) p. 84.
39. F. Marcelin, *Au gré du souvenir*, ed. A. Challanel (Paris, 1913) p. 82.
40. F. Hibbert, op. cit., p. 102.
41. D. Delorme, op. cit., p. 127.
42. The pervasiveness of this dichotomy between 'civilization' and 'barbarism' is also evident in Latin American literature. This is the central theme of the work of Domingo Sarmiento (1811–88).
43. F. Marcelin, *Choses haïtiennes*, p. 84.

CHAPTER 2: THROUGH THE LOOKING GLASS

1. Frederick Douglass, *Oration at the World's Fair* (Chicago, Jan. 1893) p. 29.
2. Frederick Ober, *In the Wake of Columbus* (Boston: Lothrop and Co., 1893).
3. William D. Boyce, *United States Dependencies* (New York: Rand McNally and Co., 1914) p. 123. The presentation of Haiti as a caricature of the civilized world at the turn of the century was not restricted to American commentators. Cf. Hesketh Prichard's *Where Black Rules White* (A journey across and about Haiti) in 1900 is equally insistent that in Haiti cannibalism flourished and that without 'the presence of the white element . . . the Republic would go sliding back into the depths of barbarism'.

4. Ludwell Lee Montague, *Haiti and the United States* (orig. edn 1940) (New York: Russel & Russel, 1966) p. 26.
5. John Houston Craige, *Cannibal Cousins* (New York: Minton, Balch and Co., 1934). Page numbers are quoted from this edition.
6. John Houston Craige, *Black Baghdad* (New York: Minton, Balch & Co., 1933). Page numbers are quoted from this edition.
7. Edward Beach, *From Annopolis to Scapa Flow* (the autobiography of a naval officer), unpublished MS, p. 241.
8. Edward Beach, *The Last Haitian Revolution* (1920), unpublished MS, p. 241.
9. Faustin Wirkus, *The White King of La Gonave* (New York: Doubleday, Doran & Co., 1931). Page numbers are quoted from this edition.
10. *Opportunity* (Jan. 1927).
11. *The Crisis* (Nov. 1935).
12. For instance, the description of Haitian culture by anthropologists such as Courlander and Herskovits in the post-war period.
13. Blair Niles, *Black Haiti* (New York: Putnam's Sons, 1926) p. 154. Page numbers are quoted from this edition.
14. Seabrook, *The Magic Island* (New York: Harcourt, Brace & Co., 1929) p. 91.
15. Price-Mars, *Une étape de l'évolution haitienne* (Port-au-Prince: Imp. la Press, 1929) p. 198.
16. Cf. Price-Mars, *La Vocation de l'Elite*.
17. John Vandercook, 'Whitewash', *Opportunity*, vol. 5, no. 10 (Oct. 1927).
18. Paul Morand, *New York* (New York: Holt & Co., 1930) p. 270.
19. Sterling Brown, 'The Negro Character as Seen by White Authors', *The Journal of Negro Education*, vol. II, no. 2 (Apr. 1933) p. 198.
20. Nathan Huggins, *Harlem Renaissance* (New York: Oxford University Press, 1971) p. 103.
21. Yvette Gindine, 'Images of the American in Haitian Literature during the Occupation 1915–1934', *Caribbean Studies*, vol. 14, no. 3 (1974) p. 41.
22. This is more fully discussed in Dash, *Literature and Ideology in Haiti 1915–61* (1981) pp. 56–9.
23. S. Alexis, *Le nègre masqué* (Port-au-Prince: Imp. de l'Etat; 1933) p. 47.
24. Leon Laleau, *Le Choc* (Port-au-Prince: La Presse, 1932) p. 207.
25. Annie Desroy, *Le Joug* (Port-au-Prince: Imp. Modele, 1934) p. 142.
26. Ibid., p. 149.
27. *La Relève* (Jan. 1934) p. 15.
28. C. L. R. James, *Mariners, Renegades and Castaways* (London: Allison & Busby, 1985) p. 44.
29. A. Rimbaud, *Oeuvres* (Paris: Garnier, 1960) p. 27.
30. *La Trouée*, no. 4 (1 Oct. 1927) p. 119.
31. *La Trouée*, no. 1 (1 July, 1927) p. 21.
32. L. Laleau, *Musique nègre* (Port-au-Prince: Indigène, 1931).

CHAPTER 3: DREAMING THE SAME DREAM

1. Nathan Huggins, *Harlem Renaissance* (New York: Oxford University Press, 1973) p. 91.
2. Paul Morand, *Hiver Carribe* (Paris: Flammarion, 1929) pp. 116–17.
3. John Matheus in *Opportunity* (Oct. 1927) p. 303.
4. Claude McKay, *A Long Way from Home* (New York: Arno Press, 1969) p. 277.
5. Mercer Cook, 'Some Literary Contacts: African, West Indian, Afro-American' in *The Black Writer in Africa and the Americas* (Los Angeles: Hennesey and Ingalls, 1973) pp. 120–1.
6. John Durham, *Diane, Priestess of Haiti* (Philadelphia: Lippincott, 1902) p. 896.
7. W. E. B. Dubois, *Correspondence 1877–1934* (Amherst: University of Massachusetts Press, 1973) pp. 212–13. Many of the incidents of the 1930s are listed in Michael Talley's M.A. thesis *The Relationship between American Negroes and Haitians* (Howard University, 1970).
8. J. Craige, *Cannibal Cousins*, op. cit., p. 78.
9. J. W. Johnson, *Along This Way* (orig. edn 1933) (New York: Viking, 1961) p. 344.
10. J. W. Johnson, 'The Truth about Haiti' *The Crisis*, vol. 20, no. 5 (Sept. 1920) p. 224.
11. Cf. Patrick Bellegarde-Smith, *In the Shadow of Powers* (New Jersey: Humanities Press, 1985) pp. 72–3.
12. *Haiti-Journal*, 26 July 1934, no. 1321.
13. L. Hughes, 'White Shadows in a Black Land', *The Crisis*, vol. 41, no. 5 (May 1932) p. 157.
14. L. Hughes, *I Wonder as I Wander* (New York: Rinehart & Co., 1956) p. 27.
15. *Popo and Fifina* (New York: Macmillan, 1932) p. 35.
16. *Opportunity*, vol. 13, no. 5 (May 1935).
17. C. McKay, *Home to Harlem* (New York: Cardinal edn, 1965) p. 145.
18. A. Locke, *The New Negro* (orig. edn 1925) (New York: Arno Press, 1968) p. 51.
19. C. McKay, *A Long Way From Home* (New York: Arno Press, 1969) p. 313.
20. E. Walrond, 'The Voodoo's Revenge', *Opportunity* (July 1925).
21. A Fauset, 'Jumby' in *Ebony and Topaz* (New York: National Urban League, 1927) p. 15.
22. Ibid., p. 19.
23. J. Matheus, 'Ti Yette' (1929) in *Plays and Pagents from the Life of the Negro* (New York: Core Collection Books). In 1949 Matheus again celebrated Haitian folk culture in his opera *Ouanga*.
24. A. Bontemps, *Drums at Dusk* (New York: Macmillan, 1939) p. 205.
25. R. Ellison, 'Mister Toussan', *New Masses* (Nov. 1941).
26. R. Hemenway, *Zora Neale Hurston* (Urbana: University of Illinois Press, 1977) p. 249.
27. Z. Hurston, *Tell My Horse* (Berkeley: Turtle Island Foundation, 1981) p. 93.

28. Other black writers such as Sterling Brown and Richard Wright objected to Hurston's politically conservative view of blacks. Cf. Hemenway, *Zora Neale Hurston*, op. cit., pp. 219 and 241.
29. M. Fabre, *La Rive Noire* (Paris: Lieu Commun, 1985) p. 190.
30. W. B. Williams, *La Relève: Focal Point of Haitian Literature*, M.A. Thesis (Washington: Howard University, 1950) p. 54.
31. M. Cassèus, *Viejo* (Port-au-Prince: La Presse, 1935) p. 14.
32. See J. Jahn, *Neo-African Literature* (New York: Grove Press, 1969) p. 274, and N. Garret, *The Renaissance of Haitian Poetry* (Paris: Présence Africaine, 1963) pp. 73–85.
33. The originality of Haitian indigenism is the subject of Michel Fabre's 'La Revue Indigène et le Mouvement Nouveau Noir', *Revue de Littérature Comparée*, no. 1 (1977) pp. 30–9.
34. Unedited Correspondence of A. Spingarn in Howard University Library.
35. L. Laleau, *La Flèche au coeur*, ed. Henry Parville (Paris, 1926) pp. 23–4.
36. Carl Brouard, *Pages Retrouvées* (ed. Panorama) (Port-au-Prince, 1963) pp. 16–36.
37. *Viejo*, op. cit., p. 66.
38. Ibid., p. 154.
39. *La Revue indigène*, no. 3 (Sept. 1927) p. 104.
40. *La Revue indigène*, no. 4 (Oct. 1927) pp. 153–4.
41. *La Relève* (1 July 1934) p. 14.
42. R. Piquion, *Un chant nouveau* (Port-au-Prince: Imp de l'Etat, 1940) p. 74.
43. *La Relève*, no. 12 (June 1933) p. 17.
44. *La Relève*, no. 3 (Sept. 1933) p. 15.
45. R. Gaillard, 'Langston Hughes, Notre Ami', *Le Nouvelliste* (26 July 1967).
46. *Haiti-Journal* (20 Oct. 1931).
47. See Carolyn Fowler's discussion of Roumain's stay in New York in *A Knot in the Thread* (Washington: Howard University Press, 1980) pp. 206–10.
48. 'Les Griefs de l'homme noir', *L'Homme de Couleur* (Paris: Plon, 1939) p. 111.
49. *Haiti-Journal* (Dec. 1945) p. 43.
50. *Gerbes pour deux amis* (Port-au-Prince: Imp. Henri Deschamps, 1945) pp. 18–20.

CHAPTER 4: PASSIONATE APOLOGISTS

1. Gunnar Myrdal, *An American Dilemma* (New York: Harper & Brothers, 1944) p. 90.
2. Franz Boas, *The Mind of Primitive Man* (New York: Macmillan, 1938) p. 271.
3. Alain Locke, 'Who or What Is a Negro?', *Opportunity* (Mar. 1942) p. 87.

4. Mabel Steedman, *Unknown to the World, Haiti* (London: Hurst & Blackett, 1939) p. 172.
5. Ruth Wilson, *Here Is Haiti* (New York: The Philosophical Library, 1957) p. 1.
6. E. Wilson, *Red, Black, Blond, Olive* (London: W. H. Allen, 1956) p. 44.
7. Ibid., p. 136.
8. M. Herskovits, *Life in a Haitian Valley* (New York: Doubleday, 1971) p. 179.
9. Ibid., p. 303.
10. H. Courlander, *Haiti Singing* (Chapel Hill: University of North Carolina Press, 1939) p. 1.
11. J. Leyburn, *The Haitian People* (New Haven: Yale University Press, 1966) p. 4.
12. Ibid., p. 295.
13. Courlander and Bastien, *Religion and Politics in Haiti* (Washington: Institute for Cross-Cultural Research, 1966) p. 40.
14. Maya Deren *The Voodoo Gods* (Frogmore: Paladin, 1975) p. 14. The original title has been made more catchy for a mass readership.
15. V. S. Naipaul, *Finding the Centre* (New York: Vintage Books, 1984) p. 90.
16. Sidney Mintz, Introduction to *Voodoo in Haiti* (London: André Deutsch, 1972), p. 2.
17. H. Cave, *Haiti, Highroad to Adventure* (New York: Holt & Co., 1952) p. 170.
18. H. Cave, *The Cross on the Drum* (New York: Doubleday, 1958) p. 172.
19. J. Leyburn, *The Haitian People*, op. cit., p. 285.
20. P. Thoby-Marcelin, *Panorama de l'art haitien* (Port-au-Prince: Imp. de l'Etat, 1956).
21. L. Rosemond, *Haiti et les Etats Unis* (Port-au-Prince: Imp. Pierre Noel, 1945) pp. 21–2.
22. B. Ormerod, 'Collapse of Stout Party: Two Haitian Views of the Anglo-Saxon Intruder', *Perspectives on Language and Literature* (Mona: University of the West Indies, 1985) p. 53.
23. A. Métraux, *Itinéraires I* (Paris: Payot, 1978) p. 148.
24. *La Relève*, no. 10 (Apr. 1937) p. 19.
25. J. B. Cinéas, *L'Héritage Sacré* (Port-au-Prince: Henri Deschamps, 1945) p. 72.
26. Ibid., p. 69.
27. Ibid., p. 67.
28. For instance F. Morisseau-Leroy in *Le Destin des Caraïbes* (1941) criticized the authenticity of Courlander's material since the latter was not assisted by a Haitian expert in the field of folk music (pp. 39–40). His later collection of creole poetry *Diacoute* (1953) mocks the American tourist and his Kodak camera.
29. Interview in *1946–1976 – Trente ans de pouvoir noir en Haiti* (Quebec: Collectif Paroles, 1976) pp. 28–9.
30. R. Depestre, *Etincelles* (Port-au-Prince: Imp. de l'Etat, 1945) p. 2.
31. J. Leyburn, *The Haitian People*, op. cit., p. 101.

32. For a discussion of some of these values see B. Ormerod, *Introduction to the French Caribbean Novel* (London: Heinemann, 1985) pp. 87–107.
33. J.-S. Alexis, *Compère Général Soleil* (Paris: Gallimard, 1955) p. 191. Page numbers are taken from this edition.
34. J.-S. Alexis, *Les arbres musiciens* (Paris: Gallimard, 1957) p. 78.
35. Ibid., p. 158.
36. J.-S. Alexis, *Romancero aux étoiles* (Paris: Gallimard, 1960) p. 208.
37. Alejo Carpentier preface to *El reino de este mundo* republished in *Chroniques* (Paris: Gallimard, 1983) pp. 348–9.

CHAPTER 5: THE ART OF DARKNESS

1. Christopher Miller, *Blank Darkness* (University of Chicago Press, 1985) p. 170.
2. V. S. Naipaul, *The Return of Eva Peron* (Harmondsworth: Penguin).
3. Ibid., p. 191.
4. M. Foucault, *The Order of Things*, op. cit., p. 48.
5. G. Greene, *Journey Without Maps* (London: Heinemann, 1953) p. 8.
6. Ibid., p. 10.
7. Ibid., p. 312.
8. F. R. Leavis, *The Great Tradition* (Harmondsworth: Penguin, 1962) p. 196.
9. M. Mahood, *The Colonial Encounter*.
10. F. Huxley, *The Invisibles* (London: Rupert Hart-Davis, 1960) p. 9.
11. G. Greene, *The Comedians* (Harmondsworth: Penguin, 1970) pp. 5–6.
12. Ibid., p. 47.
13. J. Conrad, *Heart of Darkness* (Harmondsworth: Penguin, 1976) p. 24.
14. *The Comedians*, p. 223.
15. D. Lodge, *The Novelist at the Crossroads* (London: Routledge & Kegan Paul, 1971) pp. 117–18.
16. J.-P. Sartre, *Qu'est-ce que la littérature* (Paris: Gallimard, 1948) p. 173.
17. E. Said, *Orientalism*, op. cit., p. 94.
18. Diederich and Burt, *Papa Doc* (New York: Avon Books, 1970) p. 296.
19. Ibid., p. 299.
20. Robert Heinl, *Written in Blood* (Boston: Houghton Mifflin, 1978) p. 456.
21. Ibid., p. 523.
22. R. Rotberg, *Haiti: the Politics of Squalor* (Boston: Houghton Mifflin, 1971) p. 146.
23. Ibid., p. 24.
24. A. Césaire, *Discourse on Colonialism* (New York: Monthly Review Press, 1972) p. 40.
25. H. L. Gates, *Black Literature and Literary Theory* (New York: Methuen, 1984) p. 305.
26. Ishmael Reed, *Mumbo Jumbo* (New York: Avon, 1978) p. 72.
27. Ibid., p. 72.
28. M. Foucault, *Madness and Civilisation* (London: Tavistock, 1982) p. 78.

29. J.-C. Charles, *de si jolies petites plages* (Paris: Stock, 1982).
30. Ibid., p. 21.
31. J.-C. Charles, *Le Corps Noir* (Paris: Hachette, 1980) p. 193.
32. J. Jonassaint, *Le pouvoir des mots, les maux du pouvoir* (Montreal: Arcantere et Derives, 1986) p. 258.
33. E. Roumer, *Le caiman etoileé*, ed. Panorama (Port-au-Prince, 1963) n.p.
34. F. Etienne, *Mur à crever* (Port-au-Prince: Presses Port-au-Princiennes, 1968) p. 143.
35. 'Pelin Tet: Traduction', *Conjonction*, nos 141–2 (1979) p. 80.
36. M.-T. Colimon, *Le Chant des Sirènes* (Port-au-Prince: Ed. du Soleil, 1979) p. 34.
37. Ibid., p. 78.
38. Interview with J. Jonassaint, *Le pouvoir des mots, les maux du pouvoir*, p. 89.
39. F. Etienne, *Les Affres d'un Défi* (Port-au-Prince: Henri Deschamps, 1979) pp. 1–2.
40. *Magazine littéraire*, no. 221 (July–Aug. 1985) p. 52.
41. M. Bakhtin, *Rabelais and his world* (Bloomington: Indiana University Press, 1984) p. 24.
42. *Journal d'un animal marin* (Paris: Seghers, 1964) p. 55.
43. J. Jonassaint, *Le pouvoir des mots, les maux au pouvoir*, p. 198.
44. R. Depestre, *Un arc-en-ciel pour l'occident chrétien* (Paris: Presence Africaine, 1967) p. 11.
45. Ibid., p. 13.
46. Ibid., p. 17.
47. The only full treatment of the theme of eroticism can be found in B. Jones, 'Comrade Eros: The Erotic Vein in the Writing of Rene Depestre', *Caribbean Quarterly*, vol. 27, no. 4 (1981).
48. J. Jonassaint, op. cit., p. 169.
49. J.-C. Charles, *Le corps noir* (Paris: Hachette, 1980) pp. 32–3.
50. Ibid., p. 181.
51. Ibid., p. 181.
52. J.-C. Charles, *Sainte dérive des cochons* (Montreal: Nouvelle Optique, 1977) p. 20.
53. Ibid., p. 57.
54. J.-C. Charles, *De si jolies petites plages* (Paris: Stock, 1982) p. 89.
55. Ibid., pp. 192–3.
56. Paul Rabinow (ed.), *The Foucault Reader* (Harmondsworth: Penguin, 1984) pp. 41–2.

CHAPTER 6: EPILOGUE

1. E. Genovese, *From Rebellion to Revolution* (New York: Vintage Books, 1981) p. 97.
2. Ibid., p. 88.
3. The role of the United States in the Caribbean in general and Haiti in particular is lucidly presented by David Nicholls in *Haiti in Caribbean Context* (London: Macmillan, 1985). The role of the United States in

the Caribbean in general and Haiti in particular is lucidly presented by David Nicholls in *Haiti in Caribbean Context* (London: Macmillan) 1985. An equally perceptive view of the relationship between Americans and Haitians can be found in the recent novel *Continental Drift* by Russell Banks (1985), which links the lives of a Haitian refugee and an American worker who both dream of a new life in Florida. Banks presents New World history as a series of repeated journeys and Haitians as a mysterious and exemplary community in the Americas.

Index

Africa
  nineteenth century view of, 3, 4
  Haitian links with, 32, 46
  Anti-Western response, 43
  Textualization of, 101–5
  and Haitian Revolution, 137
  see also Conrad, Greene, Naipaul,
    Rimbaud
AIDS, 134
Alexis, Stephen, 39
Alexis, Jacques Stephen, 95–100
An American Dilemma, 75
Anglo-Saxon values, 16
Anthropology, 74–84
Anti-slavery movement, 9
Antoine, Régis, 140n
Les arbres musiciens, 97–8
Arc-en-ciel pour l'occident chrétien, 127–8

Bach, Marcus, 78
Bakhtin, Mikhail, 126
Balch, Emily, 20
Banks, Russell, 147n
Barrès, Maurice, 36
Bastien, Rémy, 83
Beach, Edward, 25–7, 40
Bellegarde, Dantès, 51
Black Americans
  Haitian views of, 20–1
  Migration to Haiti, 12–14
  Harlem, 10, 34, 40, 65–6, 72, 78
  Pan-Africanism, 47
  Anti-assimilationism, 62
  and Haitian Independence, 11–13
  see also Douglass, Dubois, Johnson,
    Hurston, Hughes, Reed
Black Baghdad, 24, 27–9
Boas, Franz, 75
Boat people, 132
Body (image of)
  Animality, 30
  Romanticized, 33
  Deformed, 108
  Repossessed, 126–8
  Escape from, 130–4
Bois d'Ebène, 70
Bontemps, Arna, 58
Boyce, William, 23

Boyer, President, 13, 137
Branagan, Thomas, 6
Breton, André, 77
Brierre, Jean, 61, 113
Brouard, Carl, 43, 64
Brown, John, 19
Brown, Sterling, 10, 35
Brown, William Wells, 11, 14

Caiman étoilé, 120–1
Caliban, 44
Campbell, Joseph, 84
Cannibal Cousins, 24, 27–9
Carpentier, Alejo, 92, 100
Carroll, Lewis, 15, 22
Casseus, Maurice, 61, 64–5
Catholic Church,
  Campagne anti-superstitieuse, 87
  and the United States, 97
  Sacrilege, 43
Cave, H. B., 77, 84
Césaire, Aimé, 87, 114
Charles, Jean-Claude, 118–20, 128–34
Child, Maria, 9
Le Choc, 14–15
Christophe, Henry, 11–12, 16, 53, 136
Cinéas, Jean Baptiste, 87–91
Coicou, Massillon, 18
Colimon, Marie Thérèse, 122–4
Columbus, symbol of, 108–9
The Comedians, 106–10
Compère Général Soleil, 95–7, 99
Conrad, Joseph, 101–5
Continental Drift, 147n
Cook, Mercer, 74
Le corps noir, 129–31
corvée, 28
Courlander, Harold, 81–2, 145n
creolization, *see* race
The Crisis, 49, 51, 52
Cross-cultural imagination, 72, 100
Cuban revolution, 105, 121
Cullen, Countee, 66

Darwinism, 29, 75
Delorme, Damesvar, 17
Depestre, René, 92–4, 125–8
Deren, Maya, 78, 83–4

149

Index

Desroy, Annie, 40–1
Dessalines, Jean-Jacques, 11
Dewey, Loring, 12
Dezafi, 124–5
Diederich, Bernard, 111–12
Douglass, Frederick, 14–15, 23
Dubois, W. E. B., 48–9
Dunham, Katherine, 77
Durham, John, 48
Duvalier, François, 105–15
Duvalier, Jean-Claude, 137–8

Elite (Haitian)
  Eurocentric views, 17–18
  Critique of, 33–4
  Anti-Communism, 52
  insecurity, 85–6
  Pro-mulatto policies, 87
  Anti-élite feeling, 99–100
Ellison, Ralph, 58
Emperor Jones, 35–6
Environmentalism, 75
Eroticism, 64–6
L'espace d'un cillement, 98
Estimé, Dumarsais, 93–4
Ethnography, 74, 83
Ethnologie, Bureau d', 92
Etienne, Franck, 121, 125
Exile, 120, 122, 125

Fabre, Michel, 61
Fanon, Frantz, 119
Farrison, W., 14
Faubert, Pierre, 16
Fauset, Arthur Huff, 56–7
Female stereotypes, 3, 32, 39, 63–5
Firmin, Anténor, 16
Folk values, 55–8
Foucault, Michel, 2, 103, 118
Fowler, Carolyn, 144n
France, views of, 17, 87, 90, 138
Frazier, Franklyn, 61
Fredrickson, George, 8
Fussell, Paul, xi

Gates, Henry Louis, 116
Gaillard, Roger, 69
Geffrard, President, 12–13
Genovese, Eugene, 136–7
Gindine, Y., 37, 142n
Gobineau, Joseph-Arthur Comte de, 3, 9
Gouverneurs de la rosée, 82, 93
Greene, Graham, 101–11

Grimard, Luc, 41
Guilbaud, Tertulien, 19
Guillen, Nicolas, 92
Guillaume Sam, V., 36

Haggard, Rider, 25
Haitian Revolution
  American view of, 6–8
  Solidarity with, 11–12
  Ideals of, 137
Haiti Singing, 81–2
The Haitian People, 82, 87
Harding, Warren, 50
Harlem, *see* Black Americans
Heart of Darkness, 101–3
Heinl, Robert, 110, 112–13
Hemenway, R., 58
L'héritage sacré, 87–90
Herskovits, Melville, 55, 61, 75, 81, 99
Hibbert, Fernand, 18, 20, 37
Hippolyte, D., 66
Hoffmann, L.-F., 141n
Holly, Theodore, 13
Huggins, Nathan, 35, 46
Hughes, Langston, 52–4, 61, 66–70, 74
Hurston, Zora N., 58–60, 75
Huxley, Francis, 106

Intertextuality, 103
Indigenous movement, 62

James, C. L. R., 12, 42
Japan, 91
Jefferson, Thomas, 7
Johnson, James Weldon, 28, 49–51, 113
Jonassaint, Jean, 120
Jones, Bridget, 147n
Jordan, Winthrop, 7
Le Joug, 40–1
Journey Without Maps, 103

Kennedy, President, 110
Kristeva, 103

Laforest, Edmond, 19, 86–7, 99
Laleau, Leon, 88–9, 44, 63
Leavis, F. R., 105
Léger, J.-N., 7
Lescot, President, 74, 87, 91
Levin, Bernard, 111
Lévy-Bruhl, Lucien, 36, 75
Leyburn, James, 82, 93
Life in a Haitian Valley, 79–81
Locke, Alain, 51, 55, 62, 75–6

Index

Lodge, David, 109
Logan, Rayford, 7, 51

Mabille, Pierre, 93
The Magic Island, 31–4, 40
Mahood, Molly, 105
Mannoni, O., 114
Maran, René, 48, 57
Marbial, 78
Marcelin, Frédéric, 17, 20
Marcelin, *see also* Thoby-Marcelin
Marvellous Realism, 95, 100
Marxism, 69–70, 91, 94
Maupassant, Guy de, 109
Maurras, Charles, 35, 38
Mauvais Sang, 42, 44
McKay, Claude, 47–8, 55, 66–7
Mead, Elwood, 51
Metraux, Alfred, 84, 87
Miller, Christopher, 101
Mintz, Sidney, 84
Misreading, 69, 72
Modernist narrative, 115, 129
Mole St. Nicolas, 14, 16
Montague, Ludwell I., 24
Morand, Paul, 34, 46–7
Morisseau-Leroy, Felix, 145n
Mumbo Jumbo, 115–17
Myrdal, Gunnar, 75

NAACP, 51
Naipaul, V.-S., 83, 102
The Nation, 49
Nazism, 36
Le nègre masqué, 39
Negro colonization, 9
New Negro Movement, 62
Nicholls, David, 147n
Nigger Heaven, 84–5
Niles, Blair, 25, 31

Ober, Felix, 23
Ollivier, Emile, 124
O'Neill, Eugene, 35–6
Opportunity, 47, 51
Orientalism, 1–2, 102
Ormerod, Beverley, 87, 146n

Papa Doc, 112
Peters, DeWitt, 76
Piquion, René, 67–9
Politics of Squalor, 113–14
Popo and Fifina, 53–4
Powys, L., 30

Preece, Harold, 55
Price-Mars, Jean, 32, 40, 66, 88
Prichard, H., 141n
Priest, Josiah, 4, 33
Primitivism
 Art, 76–7
 Folk soul, 55–7
 negrophilia, 30, 35, 46
Prospero and Caliban, 114

Quixote (image of), 2, 21, 103
 see also Foucault

Race
 Cultural Darwinism, 29, 75
 nineteenth century stereotypes, 3–5, 10
 Environmental approach, 74–5
 negritude, 36, 126
 Romantic racialism, 30–3, 56–7
 Creolization, 46, 81
 see also Nazism, Ethnography, Folk
Realism, 57
Redpath, James, 9, 13
Reed, Ishmael, 115–18
Rimbaud, Arthur, 42, 104
Romantic Movement, 6
Roosevelt, President, 77
Roscoe, T., 73
Rosemond, Ludovic, 86
Rotberg, Robert, 113–15
Roumain, Jacques, 54, 56, 69, 78, 91, 93
Roumer, Emile, 120–1

Said, Edward, 1, 102, 110
St. John, Sir Spenser, 24, 105
Sartre, J.-P., 109
Schultz, George, 138
Seabrook, William, 25, 31, 59
Senghor, L.-S., 126
SHADA, 97
Les Simulacres, 37
Soulouque, Faustin, 46, 105
Spingarn, Arthur, 62
Steedman, Mabel, 76
Stowe, Harriet Beecher, 4, 9
Sylvain, Georges, 50
Sylvain, Normil, 62

Taft, Edna, 25
Talley, Michael, 143n
Tell My Horse, 58–9
Thoby-Marcelin, P., 44, 62, 77, 86
Toussaint Louverture, 6, 10, 11–12, 58

Travel writing, 30, 79, 103

Uncle Tom's Cabin, 4
L'Union Patriotique, 50
United States
  Recognition of Haiti, 8
  Southern prejudice, 8, 10
  Independence, 5, 136
  Ante-Bellum South, 27
  Anti-Communism, 111, 113
  Expansionism, 14–15
  Migration to, 122–4
  Stereotypes of, 17–19, 39–41, 86, 88–91, 127–8
  Detention Camps, 118, 132
  Occupation, 22, 44, 46, 48–50, 59, 72, 78, 85, 113

Valcin, V., 38
Vandercook, J., 30
Van Vechten, C., 34–5
Vaval, Duraciné, 39

Viejo, 61, 65
Vincent, Sténio President, 54
Voodoo
  Catholic Church and, 87
  American attitudes, 33, 80, 83–4, 112
  Harlem and, 65
  Literary use of, 42, 127

Walrond, Eric, 56
White, Walter, 51
Whittier, John, 6
White King of la Gonave, 27–8
Williams, W. B., 61
Wilson, Edmund, 77–9
Wilson, Ruth, 77
Wirkus, Faustin, 25, 27–30
Wood, Norman, 12
Wright, Richard, 57, 75
Written in Blood, 112–13

Zombi, 59, 125, 139